From Glory into Glory

From Glory into Glory

54 DAILY BIBLE READINGS
FOR LENT & EASTER

Tom Parsons

10 Publishing
a division of 10 ofthose.com

Copyright © 2022 by Tom Parsons

First published in Great Britain in 2022

British Library Cataloguing in Publication Data
A record for this book is available from the British Library

ISBN: 978-1-914966-73-6

Designed and typeset by Pete Barnsley (CreativeHoot.com)

Printed in Denmark

10Publishing, a division of 10ofthose.com
Unit C, Tomlinson Road, Leyland, PR25 2DY, England

Email: info@10ofthose.com
Website: www.10ofthose.com

1 3 5 7 10 8 6 4 2

Introduction

I have long been drawn to the later chapters of John's Gospel. They invite the attention of my adult self with the same appeal the deep end of the swimming pool held for me as a very small child. The exhilaration of diving as deep as I can into them is intensified by the awed awareness that the bottom is out of reach. I hope that as you read John 13–21 in conjunction with these daily thoughts and prayers, you will find that sense of wonder gripping you too.

These fifty-four readings have been structured to coincide with Lent and Easter. If you start on Ash Wednesday and read one per day to the end, you will be closing the book for the last time on the Sunday after Easter. Likewise you will reach John's account of Easter morning on Easter Day.

As I have written each daily section, I have assumed that the relevant Bible passage is fresh in the reader's mind. You will notice that the same biblical text is sometimes set for two or three days in a row. That's deliberate. Revisit John's narrative every day, even if you are tempted to take a short cut. Let the word of Christ dwell in you as richly as possible. And feel free to make the prayers personal, switching the 'we/us' to the 'I/me' form.

Speaking about personal matters, I'd like to give an introductory encouragement to anyone who has not yet become a committed follower of Jesus. I have written primarily for those who have taken that momentous step already. However, please read on. I hope that as you consider Jesus' words, God will bring new life to birth within you. I pray that interest will develop into understanding; that understanding might grow into conviction; and that conviction will lead to life-giving faith.

John's account of the cross first grabbed hold of me as I prepared to conduct student performances of Bach's classic, *The St John Passion*. It stunned me that Jesus viewed the cross as the hour of his *glory*. This is a perspective we will explore often. I have tried to capture its centrality in my title. The cross is not a prelude to glory; it is glory. Jesus enters into the glory of the resurrection from the glory of the cross.

In more recent years, I have had the privilege of exploring John's Gospel with my friends at Christ Church, Sidcup. These daily notes were originally written for their use. I dedicate this book to them, my dear sisters and brothers, in thanksgiving for twelve years of fellowship and love.

I have brought you glory
on earth by finishing
the work you gave me
to do. And now, Father,
glorify me in your presence
with the glory
I had with you before
the world began.

John 17:4-5

Jesus knows that his hour has come.

He had often spoken about this moment of destiny, but it always lay in the future. Now, he embraces the shame of crucifixion with three glorious purposes in mind.

First, the hour has arrived for Jesus to go up again to the Father.

His mission is in the shape of the letter 'V'. He left the heights of the Father's heavenly glory and came down to us into the depths of our need. Then, he ascended to the same exalted rank he held before.

His appointed hour – like the sharp point at the base of the V – marks both the lowest extreme of his descent and the beginning of his ascent. It is simultaneously his ground zero and his launch pad.

We are going to marvel that, in the very instant he is lifted on the cross, embracing the lowest place of a condemned criminal, he is already moving upwards on his glorious ascent to the Father.

Second, the hour has arrived for Jesus to enact God's love to the ultimate degree.

God loved the world so much that he sent his Son to bear the extreme consequences of our sin. That's the only way he could lift us into the infinite glory of the Father's presence.

Read on, then, and expect to see God's love fully outstretched as we watch Jesus love his disciples to the end (verse 1).

Third, the hour has arrived for Jesus to overcome the powers of darkness.

The way John has structured verses 1–3 makes that point clearly. He's created a sandwich. Verses 1 and 3 tell us that Jesus knew he was empowered to accomplish God's purposes. In the middle stands verse 2, informing us of the evil alliance between Satan and Judas.

John wants us to know that this destructive plot is held within Jesus' knowledge and control. As a result, it is not only doomed to fail, but to serve God's purpose.

John begins his account of the appointed hour inside Jesus' mind. To worldly eyes, the cross is shameful, hopeless and hateful. But Jesus foresees that it will be glorious, victorious and overflowing with love.

Let's read and pray through John's account over the weeks of Lent and Easter, asking that we might understand the events more deeply and embrace their significance as Jesus did.

Father God, may the Spirit, who inspired John to write, give light to our minds. As we watch Jesus return to the Father through the shame of the cross, may we see love fully expressed and darkness decisively defeated. In the name of Jesus, who embraced his hour for your glory and our salvation. Amen.

The first step on Jesus' journey up to the Father's glory leads him downwards into a close encounter with his disciples' dirty feet.

Foot washing was a task reserved for slaves. Picture Jesus there on his knees and hold the image in mind. He intends this act of servanthood to provide an explanation of what his imminent death means for us all.

Peter, the lead disciple, doesn't like what he sees. He's mortified when Jesus takes his heel in hand and attends to his toes. He protests, 'Lord, are you going to wash my feet?' (verse 6).

Peter is horrified that the usual order of things has been reversed. Lesser people serve greater people. That's just how it is in this world. So Peter stiffens his protest: '"No," said Peter, "You shall never wash my feet"' (verse 8).

Peter doesn't understand what Jesus is doing. The foot washing symbolises the greater act of service Jesus is soon to perform. By his death Jesus will provide true cleansing, washing away sin, guilt and shame.

No wonder Jesus is uncompromising in his reply. Peter must accept Jesus' service. If he refuses the symbolic washing, how will he receive the real thing? And without that ultimate cleansing, he can have no relationship with Jesus at all.

Peter doesn't yet grasp the symbolism. He's thinking too literally, as his over-enthusiastic request for a full-body bath demonstrates. The meaning of this event would only become clear with time.

Let's dwell on Peter's reluctance for a moment and examine ourselves. Do we find it easy to accept Jesus' service, submitting to the washing he provides by the cross? We need to be alert to the pockets of resistance that hold out against him from the deep hideouts of our hearts.

Pride resists the Servant's approach, asking, 'Am I really so dirty? Can I not at least have the dignity of washing myself?'

Fear shrinks back, dreading what might be exposed if Jesus is allowed to wash us too thoroughly.

Embarrassment rises within us, tinged with guilt that the God of heaven should put himself out for us.

Yet it is a perverse sense of dignity that stands against the tide of God's overflowing love. Drop any reluctance and let the Servant do his work in you.

Glorious Father, we praise you for sending your Son into the world not to be served but to serve. Forgive our reluctance to receive him. Cleanse our hearts and minds by the blood he shed for us. Renew our lives by the power of the Holy Spirit and set our consciences at rest before you. In Jesus' name. Amen.

Two verbs – doing words – leap out from this passage: to know and to do.

First, knowing.

Jesus *knows* his destination and he *knows* what authority rests in his hands. He *knows* Judas' plan too. By contrast, Peter doesn't yet *know* what Jesus is doing. Later Jesus asks if his disciples *know* what his action means.

Then, doing.

Jesus doesn't only know things; he also acts. Again, Peter doesn't understand what his master is *doing*. So later, Jesus asks if they understood what he had *done*. Finally, he commends his example for their imitation: 'I have set you an example that you should do as I have done for you' (verse 15).

The two key verbs come together in verse 17: 'Now that you *know* these things you will be blessed if you *do* them' (my emphasis).

To know and to do: in the Christian life it's vital that the two go together.

It's possible to pour out our lives in service without first knowing the joy of Jesus serving us. This *doing* without *knowing* leads to exhaustion, resentment and self-righteousness.

Or imagine the opposite. Suppose someone else knows Jesus' life-cleansing power – or thinks they do – yet makes no active attempt to serve others. Their lack of *doing* shows that they don't really *know* at all.

Not only must the two verbs be held together, they also need to be placed in the right order. Knowing comes before doing. It's the knowledge that Jesus has served us that gives us the spiritual power to serve others.

Picture a horse and cart. 'Knowing' is the horse; 'doing' is the cart. Hitching them in the wrong order results in a stationary cart, and a justifiably irritated horse!

Paul also recognised the centrality of this sequence to the Christian life. He wrote, 'The only thing that counts is faith [to know] expressing itself through love [to do]' (Galatians 5:6).

Knowing what he knew, Jesus did what he did. He did it for us. Opportunities for service will present themselves today. Knowing such great love, how can we not take them?

Father God, by the Spirit's enabling, give us the energy and imagination to serve others. May we find blessing in both knowing and enacting the glorious love of our Saviour and Lord, Jesus Christ. Amen.

Betrayal is a murky business. By its very nature, it is shrouded in a cloak of darkness.

Take, for example, the betrayal of William Tyndale, the great translator of the English Bible. In 1535, Tyndale was working undercover throughout what is now Belgium. An English student named Henry Philips gained his trust, only to hand him over to the authorities. Tyndale was tried, condemned and burned at the stake.

It is almost certain that a powerful figure in England sent Philips on his vile errand. But who? To this day, no one knows for sure. By contrast, Jesus knew all the details of his betrayal before it took place. The time had come for him to alert the disciples to the presence of a traitor.

With hindsight, they would see in this sobering announcement a clear revelation of Jesus' all-knowing divine identity (verse 19). Perhaps they could appreciate how ironic it is that Jesus demonstrated his reliability by predicting history's most famous act of treachery!

Yet at the time, the announcement is crushing. Suspicion and self-doubt now intrude. Which one of their friends is not their friend? *Or – and this is more disturbing still – maybe it's me; am I going to crack under the pressure?*

Simon Peter gets John to press Jesus for an identification. ('The disciple whom Jesus loved' in verse 23 is John's way of referring to himself.) Jesus answers, 'It is the one to whom I will give this piece of bread when I have dipped it in the dish' (verse 26).

It seems that only John hears Jesus' words and that he doesn't understand them, because when Jesus hands the bread to Judas, no one thinks anything of it. The disciples blandly note the betrayer's departure and assume that Jesus has sent him on an errand in his capacity as treasurer.

They have no idea what Jesus is setting in motion as he despatches Judas to his appointed task. He is handing Satan the opportunity to crucify him.

And they completely miss the spiritual significance of the night-time hour (verse 30). Darkness engulfs Judas as he turns his back on Jesus, the Light of the world.

Betrayal is a murky, secretive and disorientating business. But the darkness is as day to Jesus. With full knowledge, he identifies his betrayer. With selfless love, he sends him on his errand.

As we turn to prayer now, enjoy the rich benefits of hindsight. Be reassured that, no matter how the darkness threatens to overcome Jesus, his light only shines more brilliantly.

Lord Jesus, our hearts are deceitful above all things, and we dare not trust the strength of our own faith. Anchor our lives firmly to your Father's unchanging faithfulness, and shelter us under the refuge of his wing by the might of the Holy Spirit. Let us never wander from the light of your presence. For your name's sake. Amen.

Judas' departure prompts Jesus to speak about his own imminent death: 'Now the Son of Man is glorified and God is glorified in him' (verse 31). This statement seems violently at odds with the situation. How can the crucifixion of a young, innocent man be positive in any way, let alone an expression of divine glory?

The clue to solving this puzzle is the title Jesus applies to himself. This squalid execution is glorious because it is the action of *the Son of Man*.

This title belongs to a human figure introduced in the Old Testament book of Daniel (7:13–28). The 'Son of Man' is the perfect representative of God's imperfect people. He enters God's presence and receives everlasting authority, all on their behalf.

Before he enters this exalted state, the Son of Man must represent his people under the judgement they deserve. This is what Jesus will do in his suffering and death.

Crucifixion itself remains a repulsive horror. This ugliness is certainly on display in the Son of Man's execution. Yet, for those with eyes to see, a unique and vivid light radiates from his cross. The Father's glorious love towards the world shines in and through him with passionate intensity.

If Peter could have appreciated this at the time, it would have spared him from his many misunderstandings. For example, when Jesus insists that only he can walk the path ahead (verse 33), Peter disagrees. He thinks that he has what it takes to come along too (verse 37).

Kenyan athlete Eliud Kipchoge currently holds the men's marathon world record of 2:01:39. The average 100-metre split in his record-breaking run was 17.3 seconds. I can run at that pace too – for 100 metres. It would be foolish to claim I could stick with Kipchoge for the entire 26 miles.

Peter is proposing an impossibility of an even higher order. He cannot stand before the Father's throne as a fellow-representative alongside the Son of Man. He needs to be represented himself. Jesus must go alone. He cannot accomplish salvation *with* us, precisely because he is doing it *for* us.

One day Peter will follow in the path of Jesus' suffering. He will become his Saviour's persecuted ambassador. First, though, he must set aside his misguided heroism, abandon all thought of contributing to Jesus' unique work, and humbly allow the Son of Man to represent him.

Father God, we worship your Son, Jesus, whom you have glorified forever. Enlighten the eyes of our hearts by the Spirit, that we may see his glory clearly displayed at the cross. Help us to rest in what he has done for us and to follow him in dependence and with joy. For his praise. Amen.

In verses 34–35, Jesus looks beyond his death to the life of the community it will create. His followers must live by one underlying and overarching rule: 'A new command I give you: love one another' (verse 34). We will consider the command itself, and then its impact.

It is important to understand in what sense this command is *new*. After all, it is found in similar forms in the ancient Law given to Moses. I suggest that, while the command itself is not an innovation, Jesus' example has renewed it with fresh significance.

In his death Jesus acted with a love never witnessed before. The new command charges his followers to make this same self-sacrificial love the defining mark of their life together. We must give up our own interests to serve others, just as he did.

Perhaps that makes you feel overwhelmed. Relationships in our local churches often feel superficial. Our times together are frenetic and snatched. How can we possibly love one another in the way Jesus demands? While loudly affirming the importance of this command in theory, it's easier to file it quietly in the 'too hard to be practical' folder.

Don't let the new commandment crush you! It should inspire us to ask, 'Who can we serve today?' Pick up the phone to encourage a person who hasn't been in church for a few weeks. Make the visit you've been putting off. Write that card, deliver that meal or give that money.

If we hear the new commandment with only drastic acts of self-sacrifice in mind, the pressure will prove paralysing. Yet if we simply ask ourselves each day whom we can serve, we will make progress.

Indeed, the Holy Spirit tends to inspire radical acts of sacrifice in churches that are in the habit of loving one another in smaller ways.

The impact of a loving community of Christ's followers mustn't be underestimated. Observers will recognise that we are Jesus' disciples, and through us they will see him.

Perhaps, like me, you have caught yourself impatiently wishing that Jesus would demonstrate the overwhelming power of his message to a sceptical world: 'Lord, how about some miracles, a mighty evangelist or a great revival?'

But there's no need for these displays. The ultimate confirmation of Jesus' message is the love it produces among his disciples. In this cynical and unbelieving world, the proof is in the loving.

Father, forgive our self-preoccupation, through the blood of the one who gave himself for us. May his Spirit create clean hearts within us and enable us to respond creatively to the needs of others with the same patience and compassion we have received. Through Christ our Lord. Amen.

Jesus' parting instructions to his disciples fill John chapters 14–17. They combine to form what Christian tradition has labelled 'The Farewell Discourse'. I hope that by the time we get to its end you will agree that the word 'farewell' is misleading.

True, Jesus is leaving his disciples. But only so he can be more present with them than before.

Jesus begins his instructions by urging his disciples not to let their hearts be troubled. We have reason to puzzle over this. Twice in the previous two chapters we read that Jesus' own heart was troubled (12:27 and 13:21). Let's apply ourselves to this apparent inconsistency.

The disciples don't need to let themselves be troubled. Yes, Jesus is leaving them, but his journey has the most comforting purpose. He is going to prepare them a room in his Father's house, where there is space for them all.

As for Jesus, it's no wonder his heart is burdened. He must go to the Father's house *via* the cross. Dying as our representative, he will remove the condemnation that otherwise prevents us from dwelling with a holy and just God. The journey is infinitely costly to Jesus, and deeply distressing by its very nature.

However, Jesus does not want his disciples to focus on that cost or to fret about carrying a burden only he can bear. Instead, he reassures them that once the preparations are made, their place in the Father's house will be absolutely secure.

This security is a reassurance to every follower of Jesus. Yet, still, our hearts might fret. We may protest, 'But Jesus, how will we get there without you?'

Jesus has more reassurance for his disciples. He promises to 'come back and take you to be with me' (Verse 3). That will happen in the ultimate sense at the Second Coming.

There are interim comings too. He came back in the resurrection. He comes to us in the Holy Spirit. And he meets with each believer at the point of death. In every meeting, he leads us straight to the Father.

How could Jesus say 'do not let your hearts be troubled' when his own heart trembled? He was about to take upon himself the condemnation we have reason to fear. It was for him to be troubled with our griefs. It is for us to be at peace through his troubles.

Father, we thank you that Jesus' intention is to bring us into your eternal presence with all the joy of homecoming. Help us to rest in him, who was troubled in heart that we might live in peace. May our lives overflow with hope by the power of the Holy Spirit. In Jesus' name. Amen.

I was on a mission to find Decathlon, the sports store, in a large French town. Alas, the success of my assignment was in jeopardy. I was lost, due mainly to my heroic determination not to use satellite navigation. *No need to worry*, I thought. *I can ask a local for directions.*

I unleashed my school-level *Franglais* on a local woman. I tried to follow her detailed French instructions, but my face must have betrayed my true helplessness. Pointing to her car, she indicated that I should follow. Five minutes later, it was mission accomplished – all thanks to her.

Jesus informs the disciples that they know the way to the place where he is going (verse 4). Thomas disagrees. As far as he is concerned, Jesus hasn't even specified the destination. How, then, can the disciples possibly know the way?

However, Jesus has clearly told them where he is going. Thomas is confused because he expects the destination to be a place. But Jesus has spoken about going to a person, his Father.

If Thomas had twigged this, he would have realised that he did know the way after all. Careful consideration might have led him to conclude that the way to reach this unseen person must be through another person, specifically through someone who knows the Father and can secure Thomas an introduction.

That would be none other than Jesus, the Son of God!

The whole church is grateful for Thomas' misunderstanding because, in response, Jesus makes this great statement: 'I am the way and the truth and the life. No one comes to the Father except through me' (verse 6).

Jesus is the way to the Father by virtue of both who he is and what he has done. On the one hand, he is the Father's only Son, with full authority to bring his friends into the family home. On the other hand, he has taken our rightful place in death so we can live in his rightful place with the Father.

Note Jesus' language well. He doesn't claim only to point the way to the Father, nor merely to lead us to him, as that French woman led me to the shop. He asserts that he *is* the Way. We reach the destination in him. We receive the Father's truth and life from the moment we come to him.

Many people find Jesus' statement exclusive and intolerant, but that's a tragic misunderstanding. It is the opposite. He opens the Father's house to us all, regardless of what qualifications we think we possess or know we lack. Anyone may come to the Father by this one definitive way: Jesus.

Father, we come before you now in Jesus, your Son. Keep our eyes fixed on him that his truth may lighten our minds and his life energise our hearts. Give us boldness today that, in step with the Spirit, we will point others to this one great hope for all. We pray through Jesus, the Way, the Truth and the Life. Amen.

'Jesus is certainly impressive, but why can't God show himself to me?' You might have heard an enquirer into the Christian faith express that sort of frustration. The disciple Philip knows where they are coming from.

He is exasperated when Jesus says, in verse 7, 'If you really know me, you will know my Father as well. From now on, you do know him and have seen him.' Philip issues a blunt request in an attempt to cut through what he can only assume is an exaggerated figure of speech: 'Lord, show us the Father and that will be enough for us' (verse 8).

What does Philip expect Jesus to do? Perhaps he hopes Jesus might unzip the sky over his head and unveil a vision of heaven. In his exasperation, Philip longs for Jesus to offer a direct and conclusive encounter with the unseen Father.

Jesus is exasperated too. Philip's question reveals that even after three years together, the disciples are blind to the full truth about their teacher. Jesus doesn't need to point to the Father beyond himself, because the Father is fully present in him.

Philip has not grasped that the Father and the Son live *in* one another. He's unaware that, since he has seen the Son, he has encountered the Father too.

How is your brain coping? We find it hard to grasp how one divine person can be fully present in another, while remaining perfectly distinct. This has stretched the best minds God has given to his church, but no one can dodge the force of Jesus' logic.

Jesus claims that his authoritative words and miraculous works are also the Father's. When Jesus taught, healed and raised the dead, the Father was teaching, healing and giving life in and through him.

As the early church scrambled to find language to describe this reality, they settled on words that are still familiar to us today from the Nicene Creed: the Son is *of one being*, or *of one substance*, with the Father. They reasoned that, since these distinct persons share the same actions, they must share the same divine nature.

Philip thinks that, to offer a vision of the Father, Jesus needs to point away from himself to someone else. Just suppose Jesus granted his wish, unzipped the sky and pointed to the Father. What would Philip see? None other than the person he had already met and loved in Jesus.

Father God, we thank you for giving us the light of the knowledge of your glory in the face, the words and the actions of Jesus Christ. Open our eyes to see you in him. Buoyant with faith, make us witnesses to his divine identity. Through him, and in dependence on the Holy Spirit. Amen.

It's the night before Jesus' execution. We might expect him to use this time to tie up life's loose ends. However, he's about to announce a massive expansion in his mission.

Jesus began chapter 14 with words of comfort for his grieving disciples, but from verse 12 he begins to lift their eyes to the good things they can look forward to beyond his death.

For Jesus himself, a glorious transformation awaits. He will shortly pass beyond the humiliation of his death-bound earthly existence to inherit the Father's heavenly kingdom, power and glory.

Jesus' disciples will have a friend in the very highest place. As a result, an appeal to the Father in his name will give them direct access to an open and all-powerful ear. They will be granted whatever they request.

This promise has puzzled Christians. *Anything* we request? Perhaps you know the pain and perplexity of prayers that appear to remain unanswered. Be reassured that God is as merciful when he says 'no' as he is wise when he says 'wait' and kind when he answers our prayers with a resounding 'yes'.

Anything we request? That's right – so long as we keep the context of this promise in mind. Jesus' mission is expanding. He is going to work in response to his people's prayers to bring glory to the Father. As the disciples pray boldly towards that goal, Jesus will do greater works through them than they had ever seen him perform.

We may wonder how this can be true. The apostles certainly performed supernatural wonders, but can we honestly say these were greater than – for example – the feeding of the 5000 or the raising of Lazarus? While miracles do still take place at times, I suggest that Jesus did not have such signs in mind.

The works Jesus mentions will be greater *because he is going to the Father*. From that exalted place, he will send the Spirit to transform lives in regions far beyond Jerusalem and long after this moment in history.

We see this beginning to happen in Acts, as the ascended Jesus transforms lives and establishes churches throughout the Mediterranean. We will discover that he is still at work today as we involve ourselves prayerfully in world mission and local evangelism.

Heavenly Father, in the name of Jesus, your ascended Son, we pray that you will be glorified. May the Holy Spirit empower the whole church to accomplish whatever greater works Jesus has in mind for this day. Give us the joy of participating in them too. In his name. Amen.

I don't know if you agree with this age-old reassurance: 'It is better to have loved and lost than never to have loved at all.' I think it's true. I'm also thankful that Jesus had better consolation for his distraught disciples as he left them. The one they love, they will never lose.

For the next few days, we will immerse ourselves in Jesus' introduction to the work of the Holy Spirit. Today, our attention rests on the defining centre of the Spirit's ministry, which is pinpointed in verses 16-17: 'And I will ask the Father, and he will give you another advocate to help you and be with you for ever – the Spirit of truth.'

Another *advocate*. Your version might have translated the Greek word in various valid ways: comforter, or counsellor, or helper, for example. The word denotes a person who is called alongside someone else to appear or speak for them in their need. Think, for example, of a defence barrister in a criminal trial.

What will this advocate do? The word *another* gives the clue. Jesus has been the disciples' advocate until that point. Soon *another* one will come, to defend, challenge, encourage and inspire them as Jesus had.

This might be of some comfort, but I can imagine the disciples feeling like a little child who is promised a replacement for a lost toy. The toddler stamps her feet, saying, 'I don't want *another* one; I want my old one back!'

It's true that the Holy Spirit is a distinct person from Jesus, but Jesus stresses that he himself will be fully present in the person of the Holy Spirit. He confirms this in a remarkable sequence of promises, beginning in verse 18: 'I will not leave you as orphans; I will come to you.' He will come by the Spirit.

In verse 19, he indicates that, while he will be invisible to the world, there is a sense in which the disciples will see him. The Spirit will continually present him to the eyes of their hearts. More than this, the Spirit will bring the Father to the disciples too (verse 23).

Another? Yes, a distinct divine person is on his way. Yet the Spirit shares equally in the being and life of the Father and the Son. Through his ministry, we can live in Jesus' presence even though he has gone to the Father.

Can you take it in? Wherever you go today, Jesus is coming with you.

Father, we thank you for giving the Holy Spirit to your people through your glorified Son, Jesus Christ. May this mighty Advocate fill our lives today and make us constantly aware that Jesus is with us at every step, strengthening, defending, challenging and inspiring us as we go. In his name. Amen.

The Holy Spirit will come to make Jesus ever-present with his disciples.

This confronts us with an important question: how do we know that the presence we experience as Jesus really is him?

The spirit of each passing age tempts God's people to interpret Jesus according to whatever it considers relevant and valuable. Jesus has been reinterpreted as a desert hermit, for example, and as a crusader and a hippie. The church is easily duped. We experience a presence, and think it is Jesus. How can we be sure that it really is?

The same Spirit, who makes Jesus present to us, has also provided the means for us to know that the presence we experience truly is Jesus. The Spirit brings us both Jesus' presence and his history.

Jesus made provision for the preservation of an accurate account of his words and actions. He promised that the Holy Spirit would remind the disciples of everything he said and did. They wrote down these recollections, and we read them in the New Testament.

A wave of communication surges through these verses. The disciples have heard the Father's words from Jesus' lips. At the right time, the Spirit will remind them of what he said, and empower them to proclaim it to the church of the future.

As a result, every successive generation will be able to confirm that the Jesus it trusts, and experiences, is the authentic version. If the Jesus we experience is the same Jesus they preached, we can be sure that we are not deceived.

Put another way, the Holy Spirit has a two-pronged approach to delivering Jesus' presence to his people. First, he enabled the disciples to record Jesus' history accurately. And second, he makes the same Jesus we meet in the biblical narratives present to us today.

We need both gifts of the Spirit: our Saviour's history and his living presence. The history without the presence would create a dusty study group, not a church. On the other hand, without the Spirit-inspired history to regulate our experience, we would be left wide open to deceptive spiritual forces.

Praise be to the Spirit, who gives us what we need. Through him, we can step into today knowing that Jesus himself walks with us.

Lord Jesus, we praise you for the gift of your Spirit. By his power, give us both a deeper understanding of the Scriptures he has inspired, and an increased awareness of your living presence with us today. To the glory of the Father and the joy of our hearts. Amen.

The Holy Spirit will unite the disciples to Jesus. He will unite them to the Father. He is the great uniter, joining us to the love and life of God. This is a beautiful idea, which we should ponder in worship. It also carries practical implications which we are expected to implement.

As we read this text for a third day, we can't fail to notice the link between loving Jesus and obeying him:

- Verse 15: 'If you love me, keep my commands.'

- Verse 21: 'Whoever has my commands and keeps them is the one who loves me.'

- Verses 23–24: 'Anyone who loves me will obey my teaching … Anyone who does not love me will not obey my teaching.'

Real love for Jesus will show itself in lives that are increasingly shaped by his teaching. By contrast, where obedience is absent, there is no reason to think that the love we claim to have for him is anything more than a delusion.

This coupling of love and obedience rankles in our age. We are highly sensitised to illegitimate claims on our obedience. Isn't it controlling and manipulative for Jesus to require obedience as the sign of true love?

It would be exactly that in relationships between fallible, self-centred human beings. But our union with the Father, Son and Spirit is different. He is the perfectly good, all-wise God.

In addition, Jesus is not asking us to tread a path he has not already walked. He established our relationship with God by his own act of loving obedience. The Father required Jesus to pay an infinite price to bring us into fellowship with himself. Jesus gladly obeyed his will, because he loved him.

Once the Spirit has united a person to Jesus, they are expected to act like their Saviour did. His love for the Father led him to obey. Our love for Jesus must express itself in the same way.

Jesus' teaching confronts us with costly demands. He insists that we die to ourselves and put our sin to death. It can feel like self-crucifixion. If we love him, we will obey.

We may also discover that it is often in the costliest instances of obedience, that we experience our union with Father, Son and Spirit most intimately.

Father, we praise you for working through your Son and Spirit to bring us into loving union with yourself. Redirect our wills in the path of your commandments and enable us to run in it with joyful hearts. In the name of Jesus who, through love, became obedient to death on the cross. Amen.

On a recent summer holiday, we camped among some of the finest vines in Burgundy. These pristine fields wouldn't win a beauty prize at the Chelsea Flower Show, but the French farmers don't mind that. Like God the Father, they are only interested in fruit.

Jesus sets up a famous word picture by saying, 'I am the true vine, and my Father is the gardener' (verse 1). The assorted branches of the vine represent those who have gathered around to hear Jesus' word. Some are real disciples. Others are not.

The imagery is not new. Several Old Testament passages describe God's people as a vine that fails to produce the fruit God desires (see for example Psalm 80:8–15 and Isaiah 5:7). Against that background, Jesus identifies himself as the true vine: the one man who will single-handedly bear the fruit the people failed to yield.

Today, we will concentrate on the gardener who tends the vine: God the Father. He is determined that every branch will bring forth the same loving obedience that Jesus displayed.

He removes the branches that have no real connection to the vine. They are not really Jesus' disciples at all.

This might alarm you unduly. Those of us with sensitive consciences fret that perhaps we are fruitless branches. Be reassured. The very fact this concerns you is evidence that you are securely joined to the vine.

As for the branches that are connected to the vine, the Father is determined to maximise their fruit-bearing potential. How does he prune them? His tool is the word Jesus has spoken to us. It removes what is dead and transplants new life into us.

But another factor is sometimes required. To make a cut, there needs to be some pressure. Sure enough, it's often only when difficulties hit us that our false hopes, distracting habits and distorted priorities are cut away.

It alarms me when I watch expert gardeners pruning plants and trees. I feel like saying, *'Be careful you don't kill it!'* But they know what they are doing. They want to harness maximum energy for fruit growth, even at the cost of drastic cropping.

If only we could embrace the Father's purpose for the vine! We might sometimes wish that he aimed supremely for our comfort and ease. Yet fruit is better. If we keep on trusting him, we will see that soon enough.

Father God, make us fruitful branches in the true vine. Help us to embrace your purpose and to prize loving obedience as highly as you do. Give us Spirit-inspired trust in your goodness, especially when the pruning blade presses hard. In Jesus' name. Amen.

Long-distance relationships are hard work, even in an age of digital interconnectivity. Thankfully, then, our relationship with Jesus is not conducted at a distance, even though he has now gone to the Father.

Jesus says to his disciples, 'I am the vine; you are the branches' (verse 5). The branches are not merely close to the vine; they are united to it. The life of the vine is in the branches. In the same way, the life of Jesus is shared with his people through the continuous work of the Holy Spirit within them.

It is God who has established this connection. We could never 'plug in' to Jesus' life by our own ingenuity. We receive this union as a gift through simple trust in the Son, Jesus Christ.

Simple trust, however, must not be passive. Jesus instructs us actively to remain in him. In a paradox that lies at the heart of Christian living, it requires discipline and effort to rest in his grace. There must be prayer and obedience to his word, and a deliberate pursuit of his fellowship each day.

Jesus describes in absolute terms why it is so important to remain in him. It is absolutely necessary that we remain in Jesus because, he says, 'apart from me you can do nothing' (verse 5). Indeed, a branch that becomes separated from the vine isn't just fruitless; it's dead.

Sometimes, in God's wisdom, he gives us a taste of our dependence on him. John Newton, the former slave trader who became a great hymn writer and pastor, knew this:

Though my pen and my tongue sometimes move freely, yet the total incapacity and stagnation of thought I labour under at other times, convinces me, that in myself I am not sufficient to think a good thought ... for every new service, I can bring forth nothing from my supposed store, but stand in need of a new supply.[1]

Apart from Jesus, we can do absolutely nothing. Yet if we do remain in him, it is absolutely inevitable that fruit will grow. Jesus himself will produce it in us.

Feeling fruitless? Our instincts tell us to summon our strength and try harder, but that strategy usually leads to misery, and even despair. Instead, actively refuse to rely on your own efforts. Look to Jesus and ask that his Spirit will energise and enable you. Just wait and see: the fruit will come.

Father God, we thank you for the promise that, if we remain in Jesus, we will bear much fruit. Give us the Holy Spirit in abundance. May Jesus' life flow within us and through us, that you might have the harvest you desire. Amen.

---

1   From a letter to William Legge, 23 February 1775 in *The Works of John Newton*, Vol 1 (Banner of Truth, 2015) p. 368.

What is the fruit the Father wants, the fruit we will bear if we remain in Jesus?

Some have thought that it's mainly about Christ-like character, referencing the fruit of the Spirit (Galatians 5:22–23). Others consider that it refers to new converts. I suggest that we don't have to choose either one or the other of these options, because both are aspects of this precious fruit.

In the profound teaching of John 15:9–17, Jesus sets himself before us as the pattern we must follow if we are to bear fruit. We'll follow his train of thought, before attempting a definition.

Jesus remained in his Father through his loving obedience. In the same way, we must remain in Jesus through loving obedience. As we do that, Jesus' joy will become our shared experience. This will produce a joyful community which will live in obedience to Jesus' new commandment: 'love each other as I have loved you' (verse 12).

How does such an obedient and loving community come into existence? It is the fruit of Jesus' loving obedience. He laid down his life in humanity's greatest act of love, to make his enemies his friends.

As his friends, we have been made partners in his fruit-bearing business. We too must lay down our lives for one another in joyful obedience. This quality of love declares to the world that we are Jesus' disciples (13:35), and as a result the community grows.

That, roughly, is Jesus' train of thought. What, then, is the fruit? It is precisely this growing community of obedient, loving and joyful people.

This explains why we don't have to choose between defining it in terms of either godly character or numerous conversions. Both are essential to the flourishing of Jesus' new community.

Think of it this way: our local churches – when they are healthy – are both the fruit itself and the means of producing more fruit.

I hope you are playing a fully committed part in your local church. If not, here's a closing word that might be relevant.

Never let the frustrations you experience in church life make you despondent. Instead, receive the irritations as a God-given opportunity to obey Jesus' command to love the difficult person. That response *is* fruit, and it might bear more fruit still.

Our Father, we thank you that Jesus was obedient to the end, giving his life to make his enemies his friends. Energised by the Holy Spirit, may we remain in his love and display it to the world, as we serve one another with joy. To you be the glory, in the church and in Christ Jesus. Amen.

Corrie ten Boom was a Dutch watchmaker who sheltered Jews during the Nazi occupation. In her memoir *The Hiding Place*, she relates an incident from her arrest:

> *I tasted blood in my mouth. My head spun, my ears rang – I was losing consciousness. 'Lord Jesus,' I cried out, 'protect me!'*
>
> *[The Nazi captain's] hand stopped in mid-air. 'If you say that name again I'll kill you.'[2]*

Corrie knew what it was to be on the receiving end of the world's hatred towards Jesus.

A sobering principle emerges in today's reading: a church that lives in loving obedience to Jesus will tend to attract the world's hatred towards him onto itself.

Hate? We discourage our children from using this strong word. Yet, after yesterday's section in which 'love' is a prominent theme, we can't miss the extreme contrast. The word 'hate' is used seven times in only eight verses.

The world hates Jesus. By 'the world', Jesus means the system of power and values that human beings cherish in their determination to live without God.

No wonder the Son of God met such hostility when he entered this treasonous stronghold. He is the world's rightful heir, and therefore the ultimate threat to those who want to possess their corner of it for themselves.

---

2 Corrie ten Boom, *The Hiding Place* (first published by Chosen Books, 1971).

The world can't but hate Jesus. It killed him when it had the chance, hoping to get rid of him forever. His followers are a standing reminder of its failure. As a result, the world's rage against Jesus falls on the heads of those who identify themselves with him. They are reviled as traitors to the world's cause and treated with unreasonable and vicious anger.

A 2017 survey by the International Society for Human Rights found that 80% of the cases of religious discrimination across the world are perpetrated against Christians. That should come as no surprise. It simply confirms Jesus' words.

Why does Jesus tell his disciples about the hatred they can expect?

He doesn't want us to be defensive, or to develop a persecution complex, or to manipulate others using victimhood as a tool. We should love the world as God does, even if it hates us back.

Jesus alerts his disciples to this hatred so they don't give up when it comes. He wants his church in every age to know that, if they meet opposition, nothing has necessarily gone wrong. The hostility might be a sign that, in fact, they are doing something right.

> Lord Jesus, may we consider it a privilege to be known as your disciples even if the world declares that it's shameful to follow you. Comfort those who face severe persecution, that by the power of the Holy Spirit they will bear the Father's fruit in the most unlikely places. To the praise of your resurrection victory. Amen.

'One word of truth outweighs the world.' I'm inspired by this Russian proverb. It was made famous in the West when Alexander Solzhenitsyn quoted it in a speech during his exile from the Soviet Union.

Can one word of truth really outweigh the world, which appears to be moved only by money and might? It certainly can when that word of truth is the gospel of Jesus Christ, and the speaker is the Holy Spirit.

Jesus has just alerted his disciples to the opposition they will face from the world. Transferring its hatred from Jesus, it will take aim at his people. Thankfully, Jesus announces the intervention of what one commentator calls 'the great counterweight'.[3]

Here is another aspect of the work of the Holy Spirit. Not only will he comfort the disciples by bringing Jesus to them, but he will also confront the world with Jesus' message: 'When the Advocate comes, whom I will send to you from the Father – the Spirit of truth who goes out from the Father – he will testify about me' (verse 26).

The Spirit is described in four different ways in that one sentence. Jesus piles up these labels and descriptions to provide maximum reassurance to the disciples. The Spirit will come with the same sovereign authority as the Father and the Son possess.

We mustn't forget to note that the disciples also have a role to play. They must testify too. Their three-year friendship with Jesus qualifies them to declare the truth about him. But their role is secondary.

---

3 Herman Ridderbos, trans. J. Vriend, *The Gospel of John: A Theological Commentary* (Eerdmans, 1997) p. 526.

It is quite deliberate that verse 26 comes before verse 27, and it's reassuring too. The Holy Spirit's testimony is mentioned ahead of the disciples' testimony. He's in the lead. They depend on him, and not the other way around – even though his usual strategy is to press his case through them.

We might sometimes wonder how men and women whose minds are shaped by today's powerful ideologies can ever come to trust in Jesus. Indeed, without the testimony of God's great counterweight, we are powerless even to grab their attention, let alone to shift their mindset.

The Holy Spirit can accomplish all this, and more, by his irresistible power. The Father has sent him into the world to do it. That's why we must never be overawed as we face a world of unbelief. Always factor in the great counterweight, and you will never lose heart.

Father God, we thank you for the Holy Spirit whom you have sent into the world to testify to Jesus. Give us courage to add our voices to his mighty testimony today, that our friends and neighbours may come to know that Jesus is the Way, the Truth and the Life. In his name. Amen.

The first time the disciples felt the whip on their backs, they rejoiced (Acts 5:40–41). Perhaps it was the very words we consider today that held them steady.

Jesus forewarns his followers of the persecution to come. He also pinpoints where the hostility is likely to come from. The fiercest enemies will be those who oppose the message *in the name of God*. They might even launch their attack in Jesus' own name.

This is profoundly disorientating because it forces us to wonder whether, maybe, we are deceiving ourselves. Perhaps God is on our opponents' side.

As Jesus' followers, we should be quick to admit our capacity for error and pig-headedness. It's right, then, that we examine our own position in humility with the Bible open before us. And we are wise not to take part in squabbles over secondary matters and issues the word of God doesn't definitively address.

An appropriate humility is vital, but beware! There is another mindset altogether that can mimic humility to devastating effect, acting as acid on our faith.

It works like this. We are so perplexed amid the competing claims that we lose confidence in our ability to discern truth. We begin to sense that no one can know God's will for sure. Some go even further and claim that there is no such thing as truth at all.

This mindset is common in our culture. It's in the churches too. It can look like a form of humility, but it is the very opposite. It's a refusal to take Jesus seriously.

There is such a thing as truth. Jesus is the truth, and we can know him.

Jesus' story confirms that the clash between truth and falsehood is real. Indeed, the Truth was crucified by those falsely claiming to act on God's behalf. We should not be surprised when his message meets the same hostility in the name of all that is righteous and good.

If we are criticised by those professing religion and godliness, we must certainly humble ourselves and search out hearts. But if we sincerely conclude that our course is straight, let us pursue it with the same clarity of purpose with which Peter and John responded to their first flogging.

Father, give us zeal for the truth and a wise self-awareness so that – setting aside our own agendas – we will press ahead with Jesus' word in our hearts, minds and mouths. Empower us by the Spirit to endure opposition for the sake of his name. Amen.

Jesus tells his grieving disciples that it is for their good that he is leaving them and going to the Father. How, they must have wondered, could that possibly be true?

The answer lies in the gift the ascended Jesus will give them: the Holy Spirit. Only a matter of weeks later, they will see what a difference this Gift makes. Thousands will believe in Jesus as the Holy Spirit uses their preaching to shake Jerusalem.

Without the Spirit, this outcome would have been unthinkable. How can the world ever see that it needs, of all things, a crucified Saviour? Only by the power of the Spirit, who will 'prove the world to be in the wrong about sin and righteousness and judgment' (verse 8).

We have all met people who couldn't care less how they stand before the God of the Bible. However, the Holy Spirit can make this matter urgent to them.

First, the Spirit convinces people that they are sinners – whereas before he sets to work, they have no idea that to live in God's world without trusting in his Son is an offence against him.

Second, the Spirit persuades people that their own righteousness cannot overcome this offence. Jesus debunked every man-made attempt to be acceptable in God's sight. The Spirit will do the same in his absence, prompting many to receive the solution God freely provides.

Third, the Spirit alerts people to coming judgement. Jesus' death condemned Satan, who is 'the prince of this world' (verse 11). This dooms the condemned prince's world to judgement too.

Many are oblivious to these three realities: sin, righteousness and judgement. Yet the Spirit highlights them, as matters of urgency, prompting even the most unlikely people to put their trust in Jesus.

The Spirit's conviction mustn't be confused with a general sense of remorse, shame and regret that leads only to hopelessness, self-pity and fear. True conviction tends to be specific, exposing distinct sins. And it comes with an element of hope, because as the Spirit shows us our need, he also points towards our only Help.

All progress in evangelism, and in the Christian life, depends on this ministry of the Spirit. Charles Spurgeon describes our utter dependence vividly.

> *Suppose a blacksmith was sent for to mend some broken iron vessels, and told that he must do it without fire. Sinners' hearts are that hard and cold. It's foolish to think that hammering at them will convert them. No! Heat the iron, and it may be mended and remoulded. Melt the soul with the Spirit of fire, or we are without hope of seeing any saving change.*[4]

Lord Jesus, increase our faith in your promise of the Spirit's conviction. May he work with more power than ever before in our hearts, our churches and the lives of everyone around us. Bear more fruit through us by the working of his irresistible power. To the glory of the Father. Amen.

---

4 Cited in comments on John 16:8 in *The Biblical Illustrator*, ed. Joseph Exell (quotation abridged).

Sometimes we learn more about a person from the tributes at their funeral than we ever knew before they died. Jesus' friends will know him better after his departure too.

Yesterday, we considered one reason it is for the disciples' good that Jesus goes away. Today, another reason: the Holy Spirit will lead them into 'all the truth' (verse 13) about the meaning of Jesus' words and actions.

This promise applies most directly to the first disciples. Jesus will lead *them* into all truth. We, who follow Jesus afterwards, need to rely on the truth entrusted to them. The Spirit leads us into all truth indirectly, as he opens our eyes to see Jesus in the writings of these foundational figures.

On the night Jesus makes this promise, the disciples are not fit to teach anyone. They are too mentally burdened to grasp the meaning of the traumatic events unfolding around them. Yet Jesus doesn't need to force the whole truth into their troubled minds. The Spirit will teach them once the crisis is over.

All the disciples need to know now is that the Spirit is a dependable teacher. That's why Jesus emphasises the perfect unity that exists between himself, the Holy Spirit and the Father.

The Spirit will speak nothing beyond what Jesus wants him to say. He will pursue no goal other than Jesus' glory. The Father has entrusted everything to the Son, and the Spirit will deliver all that truth to the disciples – whole, entire and perfect.

Put another way, Jesus is the source of what the Spirit says (the Spirit listens to him); Jesus is the content (the Spirit speaks about him); and Jesus is the goal (the Spirit glorifies him). Jesus and the Spirit are distinct persons, yet they work in unbreakable union.

The disciples can rest assured that the Spirit will give them Jesus, direct and undiluted. And we can be confident too. As we read their writings in the New Testament, we are hearing Jesus' voice.

Perhaps you have encountered Christians who think that Jesus' words have more authority than the apostles' teaching. They are mistaken. The Son and the Spirit are indivisibly united. We can be sure, then, that Jesus is the source of everything the Spirit inspired the New Testament writers to say.

Father God, we long to know Jesus better. Enlighten our minds by the Holy Spirit, and make our hearts burn within us as we understand the biblical testimony to his life, death and resurrection. Bind us to yourself, great Father, through this interlocking ministry of your Son and Spirit. In Jesus' name. Amen.

When reflecting on the disciples' many confusions, it's tempting to look down on them. Such is the privilege of hindsight. We would have been as confused as they were if we had been in the room when Jesus said, 'In a little while you will see me no more, and then after a little while you will see me' (verse 16).

It's baffling. The disciples know Jesus is going to be killed, so how can they ever see him again? And what does he mean by the phrase 'after a little while'? How long is that? Nothing makes sense to them.

We shouldn't criticise their confusion. Commentators still discuss which events Jesus had in mind: is it his departure in death and return in the resurrection; or his departure to the Father and return by the Spirit; or his physical return at the Second Coming?

But the gist is clear. There will be short-lived grief at Jesus' absence followed by never-ending joy in his presence. Whatever the imminent night brings, rejoicing will come in the morning (Psalm 30:5).

The disciples' experience will mirror that of a mother. During labour, the pains are all-consuming. Yet those fraught hours fade in memory as the joy of the baby fills her life for the weeks, months and years afterwards.

In keeping with the same pattern, the disciples will know intense grief as Jesus is crucified. However, joy will catch light within them, only thirty-six hours later, when they see Jesus again on Easter Sunday. Nothing will take away that joy.

It's true that Jesus does leave them again in his ascension. But that departure makes possible for them an even closer connection to him than before. During this 'absence', they will pray with more impact, and he will show them more of the Father than ever.

But one day this bodily absence will be over. Jesus will physically return, engulfing all his people's sorrow in jubilant praise.

So let there be joy! The grief of the cross has led to the gift of Jesus' abiding presence with his believing people now, and to the pledge of even greater rejoicing in the morning.

Lord Jesus, seated at the right hand of the Father in heaven, we believe that you are also present with us in the person of the Holy Spirit. Increase our awareness that you are within us and beside us. As we believe, fill our lives with a joy that overcomes all our fears. For the glory of your name. Amen.

A change is about to take place in the disciples' relationship with Jesus. Their earthly companion will soon become their heavenly mediator.

When Jesus was with them on earth, they asked him for everything they needed. However, when he goes to the Father, they will no longer ask him (verse 23). If they want something, they will ask the Father.

A generation ago, Tom Smail, the Scottish church leader and teacher, wrote a famous book called *The Forgotten Father*. He was convinced that many Christians neglect the first person of the Trinity. I wonder if we too are in danger of forgetting the Father.

Jesus is supremely focused on his Father, whom he frequently identifies as the source and goal of his mission (verse 28). Relationship with the Father is the highest privilege Jesus himself knows, and it's the supreme prize he offers to us.

Jesus longs to teach his disciples more about the Father, but these revelations must wait (verse 25). On that disorientating night it is enough for him to teach them one basic truth: they will pray to the Father *in his name*.

I wish I had my own story about how I used a powerful friend's name to gain privileged access into somewhere exciting. Alas, I don't. But we all understand the principle. By using the name of an esteemed person, we hope to be received in accordance with their status.

Jesus urges us to use his name to access the Father. He promises that when we do, the Father will be delighted to receive us. He will welcome us gladly, in accordance with the infinite pleasure he takes in the person and work of his Son.

This is pure good news. And yet we could take it in quite the wrong way. Perhaps the fact we need to use Jesus' name implies that the Father himself is reluctant to admit us. Does Jesus have to grovel on our behalf to persuade him of our case?

Far from it. Verses 26–27 reassure us: 'I am not saying that I will ask the Father on your behalf. No, the Father himself loves you …' The Father is the one who gave us Jesus in the first place. It was his initiative to reconcile us to himself.

Consider, then, that your company is wholeheartedly requested in heaven's highest and holiest place.

Father God, increase the depth of the Spirit's work within us. Give us unshakable assurance of your love and the fullness of joy in your presence today. In the name of your Son, our Saviour, Jesus Christ. Amen.

Fear is a mugger. Seizing our attention and removing God's word from our minds, it snatches our peace and strips from us all hope of getting it back again.

Are you troubled in heart? I urge you, right now, to exert all the mental energy you can muster and to tear your attention away from whatever is making you afraid. Concentrate instead on Jesus' reassuring words, which are stronger and more substantial than what you dread: 'I have told you these things, so that in me you may have peace. In this world you will have trouble. But take heart! I have overcome the world' (verse 33).

It should be a comfort to us that Jesus knows about the troubles of this world. Our distressing situation may feel like uncharted territory, but it's well within Jesus' field of awareness. He knows the terrain beneath our feet and will not let us fall.

Thankfully, Jesus' promise of peace is not designed for a fantasy planet where life is easy. He gives it to this turbulent world where it is so desperately needed. It is this world he has overcome – this hard-edged, cut-throat, no-guarantee, death-bound domain.

We might wonder how Jesus can claim to have overcome the world. Within twenty-four hours of making this assertion, the 'victor' will lie in the grave, apparently defeated by a world that has no place for him.

The forces of evil were deceived. They had no idea that every step they took against Jesus further sealed their own defeat. In lifting Jesus up on the cross, they were unintentionally serving God's purposes. They inadvertently caused him to be glorified.

That hints at the vast margin of Good Friday's victory: Christ's enemies serve him, while working against him with all their might. Then comes the resurrection, which irreversibly seals the rout.

Perhaps fearsome difficulties confront you. Jesus summons you to take heart. He has overcome these troubles. Ultimately, they can only serve your good. He will transform them, in time, into channels of God's power and grace in your life.

Don't let fear mug you. Instead, let Jesus' words be the rock beneath your feet as you step into today with his peace in your heart.

Heavenly Father, forgive our fearfulness and, by your Spirit, replace it with repentance, rest, quietness and confidence. Give us peace through the victory Jesus has won and by the word he has spoken. In the name of the victorious Christ, our Lord. Amen.

The seventeenth-century puritan Thomas Manton preached a series of thirty-two sermons on John 17. In the 1950s, Dr Martyn Lloyd-Jones expounded it in forty-eight messages. We will cover this profound chapter – the Bible's Marianas Trench – in seven reflections over the next week.

Knowing that the appointed hour of death is upon him, Jesus prays, 'Father, the hour has come. Glorify your Son, that your Son may glorify you. For you granted him authority over all people that he might give eternal life to all those you have given him' (verses 1–2).

A person is glorified when what is most wonderful about them is displayed. Yet, surely, crucifixion exhibits nothing but shame and humiliation?

The Roman statesman Cicero wrote, 'The executioner, the veiling of heads, and the very word "cross," let them all be far removed from not only the bodies of Roman citizens but even from their thoughts, their eyes, and their ears.'

The naked, disjointed and bloodied body of a crucified person provokes horror. How, then, can Jesus look upon this death as the hour of his glory?

It's partly because the cross will accomplish a glorious outcome: the gift of eternal life to all Jesus' friends. More than that, at Calvary, God's character is on full display.

The Father's love has never shone more brightly than when he gave his Son to die for us. At the same time, his justice is supremely revealed. He enacts it at infinite cost to himself, refusing to disregard our sin, but paying the price to forgive it justly.

Likewise, Jesus' love shines out as he gives his life for his friends. His authority is revealed too, as he powerfully accomplishes the world's salvation from a position of abject weakness.

God has never expressed his character to us so completely as in the hour of Jesus' death.

At the cross, the splendour of God's eternal brightness shines with full intensity. Yet it is diffused through dark clouds, colouring the scene below with a strange, but captivating tint.

This vivid shade produces a remarkable effect. It inverts our perception. It causes us to interpret the scenes of Jesus' suffering in the same way we view a photographic negative.

In a negative, the colours are reversed. We see black, but we realise that the real colour is the very opposite. In the same way, when we see darkness at the cross we can sure that the light shines.

We need to readjust our eyes to perceive this unique effect. Power is revealed in Jesus' death, but it's visible in what appears to be weakness. Wisdom is displayed in apparent foolishness, and glory blazes out from the depths of shame.

Father God, we confess that the values of this world meet with deep approval in our proud minds. Forgive us, we pray, and enlighten the eyes of our hearts by the Spirit to perceive true glory in the hour of Jesus' death. In his name. Amen.

The Father has sent Jesus to gain eternal life for all his people.

What is eternal life? Here's how Jesus defines it: 'Now this is eternal life: that they may know you, the only true God, and Jesus Christ, whom you have sent' (verse 3).

Some people are horrified at the idea of eternal life because they find this life so hard to bear. Let them be reassured: the Bible teaches that Jesus' people will receive new bodies one day. These will give us endless joy, not everlasting joint pain!

Fascinatingly though, Jesus' definition of eternal life doesn't mention its duration. It makes no reference to the resurrected body we will possess or to the perfect world we will inhabit. These are uplifting realities, but not the heart of the matter.

Jesus defines eternal life in terms of relationship. It's a matter of knowing the Father and the Son.

By *knowing* the Father and the Son, Jesus doesn't just mean knowing about them, or even acknowledging that they are real. Knowing them means living in joyful and loving union with them. If we are related to the Father and the Son like that, we have eternal life now.

Deep down, most of us are aware that it's our relationships that make life *life*. Existence feels more like a living death when key relationships are rotten. On the other hand, when family connections and friendships are strong, we have an inbuilt sense that they should never come to an end.

This is to be expected. We are relational people, made in the image of a relational God. He exists in three persons: the Father, the Son and the Holy Spirit. Each one enjoys perfect knowledge of the others. We are designed to live in fellowship with this God.

Sin has broken our life-giving connection with him. As a result, we are dying even while we live. Left unchecked, our disconnection will lead to an everlasting state of death.

Jesus came to re-establish fellowship. As we put our trust in him, his Spirit gives us new birth into life-giving union with himself and with the Father. We come to *know* them and, as a result, we begin eternal life now. Death will only bring us into a fuller enjoyment of what is already ours.

Father, we thank you for your love that sent Jesus to die for us and to lift us into fellowship with yourself. Help us to know you better so that, taught by the Holy Spirit, we will share in the peace and joy of your eternal life today and forever. For Jesus' glory. Amen.

Jesus embraces his death as the starting point of a journey that leads from glory into glory. Or at least that's how he prays for it to work out: 'I have brought you glory on earth by finishing the work you gave me to do. And now, Father, glorify me in your presence with the glory I had with you before the world began' (verses 4–5).

In the crucifixion, the Son will glorify the Father. Securing eternal life for all his people, he will complete the work the Father has entrusted to him.

Beyond that, Jesus has his eyes fixed on another expression of glory. He prays that he will be readmitted to the glorious existence he enjoyed with the Father before the world began.

We mustn't miss the immense significance of this prayer. We can draw it out by highlighting a puzzle and then solving it.

Here's the puzzle: it is in the very nature of God the Son to live in his Father's glorious presence. Why, then, does Jesus ask the Father for readmittance into that state?

Here's the stunning truth. Jesus will not return to his position as he was when he left it. Then, he was solely the divine Son of God. Now, he is the divine Son of God made *flesh*. He requests admittance into the Father's glorious presence as the human being.

And not just any human being. This man, Jesus, is the Son of Man, the representative of all who put their trust in him.

It is for us that Jesus undertakes the entire journey from glory to glory. He is acting for all his people when he glorifies the Father on the cross. And it is in union with us that he now asks to be readmitted into the glory of God's eternal life.

All our ultimate interests are tied up in the outcome of this momentous request. If the Father finds Jesus' work for us complete, and duly answers his prayer, we can rest assured because we are guaranteed the same welcome with the Father as Jesus received.

It's possible that you are one of the many followers of Jesus who struggle to believe that God genuinely welcomes and embraces them. You sense that you are deeply unacceptable to him. But our own acceptability is beside the point. It's Jesus' acceptability that counts, and of this there can be no doubt.

The Father has demonstrated that he accepts Jesus' work. He has answered his Son's prayer with an unambiguous 'yes', by raising him from the dead. Emphatically confirming that our representative is welcome in the highest place, he has declared that we are welcome there too.

All glory to you, Christ Jesus, Son of God and Son of Man. We praise you for finishing the work the Father gave you to do. By the Spirit's presence, reassure our hearts that we belong, through you, in the glory you shared with the Father before the world began. To the praise of your name. Amen.

Wasabi is one of the fussiest of all plants. This hot, green stuff we eat with sushi demands a highly specific environment with precisely the right levels of light, water and soil acidity.

No one would dream of establishing a wasabi farm in a desert. Yet Jesus planted his church in still more hostile soil. It took root in the city that crucified him. It's a miracle it wasn't destroyed in the first generation.

That first generation was vital. Jesus chose these disciples to lay the foundations of the faith for all who come after them. It was essential that this group remained intact, neither crushed by persecution nor splintered by disagreement. So having prayed for himself, Jesus prays extensively for these underqualified and overburdened men.

Two related requests fill the first part of his prayer for them, in verses 6–12.

First, Jesus prays for their security: 'protect them by the power of your name, the name you gave me' (verse 11). They are to be protected by the Father's 'name', the name he gave Jesus too.

What name does Jesus have in mind? In the Bible's thinking, God's 'name' stands for his whole character. The Father's characteristics of love, power, faithfulness and holiness – and all his perfect qualities – are shared fully with Jesus. From now on, they will surround the disciples as a stronghold.

Second, Jesus prays for the disciples' unity: 'that they may be one as we are one' (verse 11). Misunderstandings and disputes certainly did threaten the early church, as the book of Acts relates. Yet Jesus' prayer holds it together in that crucial first generation.

The Father answered Jesus' prayer for unity in a tangible way. We hold it in our hands today. It's the New Testament. There, we hear the apostles' different voices and emphases combining to form one unified testimony to Jesus.

A wasabi farm in the desert? Founding the church in the city that crucified Jesus was even less promising. Jesus' prayer makes all the difference.

Father God, help us hold fast to the testimony of Jesus' first disciples. As you protected them by your name, guard their message against every attack mounted against it in our day. Help us to declare it boldly and unitedly in the power of the Holy Spirit. In Jesus' name. Amen.

The world behind me, the cross before me …
No turning back, no turning back.[5]

These words of searing commitment depict Jesus' attitude as the cross approaches. And they encapsulate the wish he expresses for his disciples in prayer: 'Sanctify them' (verse 17).

The same word soon comes to prominence again. Jesus is going to sanctify himself for the disciples that they too may be truly sanctified (verse 19). What does he mean?

To be sanctified is to be set apart and given over to God's purpose. In offering himself on the cross, Jesus not only dedicates himself to living and dying for the Father's purpose, but also devotes his followers to doing the same.

For Jesus, for his first disciples and for all his people, the cross is a border post. On one side stands the world; on the other, the love, joy and peace of God. Once we have passed that post, there must be no turning back.

Being sanctified inevitably has a negative aspect. While Jesus' followers remain in the world, we are no longer 'of the world' (verses 14–16). We reject its self-promoting values and agenda. We may live among its dazzling lights, but the world is crucified to us, and we to the world (see Galatians 6:14).

---

5 'I have decided to follow Jesus', a traditional Indian hymn, attributed to S. Sundhar Singh.

Why must the break be so ruthless? There is a positive purpose. We are set apart *from* the world to be given over *for* God's purpose. That purpose is to go into the world to continue Jesus' mission (verse 18).

We may wonder how we could ever muster up the spiritual energy required for this radical sanctification. Thankfully, though, we don't have to generate it ourselves. Jesus asks the Father to sanctify his followers 'by the truth', the truth that God has spoken in Jesus (verse 17).

As we go on listening, believing and obeying, we must expect God to use the biblical word to shape us to serve his purposes more wholeheartedly and usefully.

The world seems to exert overwhelming power as it tempts and threatens. But by his shed blood and living word, Jesus empowers his people to turn their backs on it all and to live, and to give, their lives for God.

Father God, your Son sanctified himself that his people might be truly sanctified. Let us share fellowship in his sufferings that we might live his life today. Break the spell of this world's gods so that, by the Spirit's energy, we can serve your purpose usefully. In Jesus' name. Amen.

Jesus has prayed for himself and for his grieving disciples. Now, he prays for all those who will believe their message in the future. That's us, his church. The central thrust of the prayer is clear: he repeatedly prays for our unity.

What sort of unity does he have in mind? That's an important question because – as church history shows – the wrong kind of unity does a lot of harm. For example, enforced conformity looks like unity, but it crushes people. Beware the Inquisition!

In reaction against such authoritarianism, our era offers a vision of togetherness that appears warm and cuddly. No questions will be asked and no judgements will be made. Ironically, however, this idealism creates its own authoritarian demand: everyone must accept the truth that no one knows what is true.

The unity Jesus prays for has three distinguishing characteristics.

First, it is unity with one another in the apostles' teaching, which is preserved in the New Testament. It is their message that forms the church in the first place. We foster true unity when we sit humbly together under their testimony.

Second, Jesus prays for unity in the work of God. This is what he means by phrases like, 'May they also be in us … I in them and you in me' (verses 21 and 23). In John's Gospel, Jesus expresses his oneness with the Father by accomplishing his work. We promote true unity when we work together with the Father and the Son.

Third, true unity will inevitably show Jesus to the world. The world will surely see him, as the church unites in the apostles' message and shares together in the work of God.

Suppose Jesus' prayer was fully answered today. What difference would that make to the contemporary church? I confess to feeling overwhelmed by the complex issues that question raises.

Let's keep it simple and ask ourselves one personal question: am I at one with Jesus in this prayer? We might be tempted to wish he had prioritised something else. We inwardly groan, 'Unity, with *those* people?' And that's not even looking beyond our own local fellowship!

Jesus prayed for the unity of his people. Let's join him, offering ourselves as agents of the unity he desires.

Father in heaven, forgive the self-righteousness and the hardness of heart that keeps us from loving our fellow believers. Set us free by the power of the Spirit to sit humbly with them under the apostles' teaching and to share with them in your work. That Christ might be displayed to the world. Amen.

'What's in all this for God?' That was a question a friend of mine asked on a recent course for people looking into the Christian faith. Why did God go to all the trouble of redeeming the world? There are various valid answers, but I opted for a single word response: *you*.

As we reach the end of Jesus' prayer, he expresses the desire of his heart: 'Father, I want those you have given me to be with me where I am, and to see my glory, the glory you have given me because you loved me before the creation of the world' (verse 24).

Jesus wants to be with his people. Everything he has said and done is motivated by this determination to live in fellowship with us – right now and forever.

Verse 24 points to his final goal. To use a sports metaphor, Jesus wants to show his people his 'home' glory.

On earth, Jesus has been playing 'away'. He wears his away kit. He displays glory, but it is demonstrated before the hostile crowd at Golgotha.

How different his glory will look at his home ground! Lit by the floodlight of the Father's unveiled love, he will shine with the glory he exuded before the world began. Jesus wants his followers to see him in that state and to share this inexpressible joy with him.

Before reaching this final goal, his followers have a mission to accomplish in the world. Jesus wants to be with us every moment: 'I have made you known to them, and will continue to make you known in order that the love you have for me may be in them and I myself may be in them' (verse 26). He is leaving the disciples physically, but his presence and his work among his people will continue through the Holy Spirit.

We have been considering Jesus' climactic prayer requests. He wants to be united in fellowship with his people. That prompts us to ask whether our highest desire mirrors his: do we long, more than anything else, to be with him?

Existence has no greater prize than his presence. Seek to know it today, set all hope on enjoying it fully in the future, and our hearts will come into perfect alignment with his own.

Lord Jesus Christ, we want to know your presence today. And may the Holy Spirit grip our hearts with the joyful expectation of our ultimate union with you in your Father's presence. For the glory of Father, Son and Holy Spirit. Amen.

In the year 2000, the National Gallery hosted a major exhibition of images of Jesus called *Seeing Salvation*. I was struck by how many of the paintings portrayed him as a contorted victim. It seemed to me that a number of the artists had intended to arouse pity and guilt in the viewer.

Is that how God wants us to respond as we read the narrative of Jesus' sufferings?

Jesus certainly suffers, intensely, but he is never a helpless victim to be pitied. He acts in sovereign freedom throughout. This is clear to see at his arrest.

Most people try to avoid arrest but, after the supper, Jesus deliberately goes to one of his regular meeting places. This makes it easy for Judas and the soldiers to find him (verses 1–2).

The point of an arrest is to detain someone against their will. Usually, the authorities ask the questions. Jesus' 'arrest' is very different.

The soldiers arrive looking imposing enough (verse 3), but Jesus does their work for them. He steps out from among the olive trees and questions them: 'Who is it you want?' (verse 4).

When they say his name, Jesus willingly identifies himself. He responds with an echo of the divine name revealed to Moses: 'I am'. At his words, the armed men are pinned to the floor.

The Father is glorifying Jesus, in partial answer to an earlier prayer (see 17:1). He momentarily reveals the reality that is otherwise veiled in Jesus' human flesh: this man is fully divine. It's only a fleeting flash, but it's enough to make the soldiers cower.

Farcically, Jesus needs to question them again: 'Who is it you want?' (verse 7). When they name him, he states the terms on which they may arrest him. Yes, he will yield himself to them, but the disciples must be left to go free (verse 8). Astonishingly, the arrest squad meekly agrees.

Jesus is the master of events, not their victim. He is offering himself in sovereign power and perfect freedom for the glory of his Father and the salvation of his people.

Does he call forth pity and guilt? We ought to be humbled, repentant and eternally thankful. But there's no reason for pity, as if Jesus was a helpless victim. He is the sovereign God. And there is no need for guilt. Jesus gladly gave himself for us to set us free. His self-sacrifice is best honoured when we receive this freedom with confidence and joy.

Father God, we thank you for giving all authority to your Son, and for his willingness to use it for our salvation. Give us eyes to see his active power at work through his suffering, that our hearts might receive its benefits with joy and confidence. In the power of the Spirit and the name of Jesus. Amen.

A few years ago, I was warming up my woefully unfit body before a cross-country race. Another of the runners stretching nearby had competed in the most recent Olympics. To my mortification, one of my young sons opened his mouth and, in an outburst of misguided pride, declared, 'My Dad's faster than a bullet!'

Peter is the ultimate example of an enthusiastic, but misguided, supporter.

Jesus is stepping deliberately towards the cross, but Peter's zeal flares up in a foolhardy attempt to stop him in his tracks: 'Then Simon Peter, who had a sword, drew it and struck the high priest's servant, cutting off his right ear. (The servant's name was Malchus)' (verse 10).

Jesus has allowed himself to be arrested on the condition that the soldiers let his disciples go (verse 8). This is a partial fulfilment of his earlier promise that he would not lose even one of those the Father had given him (6:39).

But no sooner has Jesus secured the disciples' safety, than Peter endangers himself. His lunge with the sword could so easily have sparked a violent response. How is it that Peter was not arrested immediately? Jesus is protecting him.

As Peter stands there, sword in hand, Jesus rebukes him. In attempting to prevent Jesus' suffering, Peter opposes God's purpose: Jesus will 'drink the cup' the Father has given him (verse 11).

'The cup' Jesus refers to is an Old Testament image for judgement (see, for example, Isaiah 51:17 and 22). The wrathful judgement of

God is pictured as foaming wine in a goblet. The guilty must drink it to its dregs.

Jesus is committed to draining that cup himself, drinking it for his people so they don't need to taste even a sip. If Peter had foreseen this glorious outcome, surely he would have done nothing to prevent it.

The arrest demonstrates Jesus' determination to embrace the cross. His enemies don't need to push him towards it because he goes of his own accord. And his friends can't stop him either, despite Peter's embarrassingly misguided zeal.

Lord Jesus, have mercy on us when our efforts to serve you thwart rather than further your purpose. Increase our zeal, directing it by your Spirit of wisdom and understanding. Make us truly useful to you today. To the Father's glory. Amen.

Jesus is taken, bound, from the olive grove to the high priest's residence. Peter heads in the same direction, with catastrophic consequences that we will consider tomorrow. Today, we meet the high priest's family.

Taken together, the Gospels record seven interrogations and trials during that night. What John describes here seems to be an informal hearing aimed at establishing some facts before the actual trial.

Yet facts are of little interest in the high priest's palace.

The interrogator is Annas, the father-in-law of the sitting high priest, Caiaphas. Perhaps he is the family grandee, the unofficial power broker who pulls the strings behind the scenes. Whatever his exact role, his influential family has already made up its mind about Jesus.

Caiaphas had already stated his view publicly (verse 14). He feared that Jesus' rising popularity might provoke the Romans, sparking a violent crackdown against the whole Jewish people. In his view, it was wisest to eliminate the rabble-rouser (11:49–51). Jesus had no chance of a fair trial from the start.

Annas asks Jesus 'about his disciples and his teaching' (verse 19). Jesus doesn't oblige him. Why should he? Jesus taught in public. He points out that there are thousands of witnesses Annas can consult if he really wants to know (verses 20–21). It seems Annas doesn't.

John's readers shouldn't be surprised that Jesus offers Annas so little. In Chapter 12, after the Jewish authorities had persistently rejected his teaching, Jesus declared that he would say nothing more to them (12:35-36). His refusal to answer Annas is in line with this earlier pronouncement.

A thuggish official strikes Jesus, indignant that he refuses to answer. In response Jesus asks a question that lays Annas' corruption bare: why strike out in violence against a statement of truth? Jesus' accusers are at war against the truth. They have prejudged the case.

Yet the sobering reality is that this case has been prejudged by the defendant as well as by the prosecution. Jesus has given his enemies many reasons to believe the truth and receive his light, but they have rejected them all.

They have prejudged him, and he them. In the immediate future this makes Jesus' death inevitable. But in only a few days it will become clear that this trial does not determine Jesus' fate. It confirms theirs.

Father God, give us a love of truth by the Spirit of truth. Put in our hearts an unwavering confidence that every force ranged against your Son, Jesus Christ, will fail. And stand by the side of those who face prejudice for the sake of his name today. For his glory. Amen.

Peter's denial is the church's most famous discipleship disaster – a manual on how to fall flat on our faces in the Christian life.

We can trace Peter's fall to his attitude earlier at the supper. Twice Jesus said to his disciples, 'Where I am going, you cannot come' (13:33 and 36). Peter refused to accept this, out of hurt pride as much as love. He promised that he would lay down his life for Jesus – which is ironic when the whole point is that Jesus must lay down his life for Peter.

Peter remains undaunted even after Jesus predicts the coming denials (13:38). He lashes out with his sword against the arrest squad, only to earn another rebuke from his Lord.

Peter thinks he knows a better way to follow Jesus than to trust and obey. It feels exhilarating and heroic to him. In fact, it is the way of unbelief, disobedience and self-confident pride.

The fact is that he shouldn't have been anywhere near the high priest's courtyard. After Jesus secured his safety (18:8), he would have been wiser to stay clear of danger. As it is, he sallies forth, without the shield of faith, into enemy territory. It takes only three puny blows to flatten him.

First, a servant girl questions him. He falls. Next, those gathered around the fire for warmth quiz him. He falls. Finally, one of the high priest's servants presses him. He falls for a third time. Immediately, the cock crows, in fulfilment of Jesus' warning.

Peter's many failures stem from a refusal to accept that the cross is at the heart of God's plans. He will not see that Jesus has work to do there which he must accomplish alone. His pride will not let Jesus do something for him, to which he contributes nothing.

Those of us who are instinctive activists can unwittingly slip into Peter's way of thinking: just try to stop us saving the world, fixing the church and rescuing everyone around us!

We need to be reminded of the old pastoral one-liner: 'Hadn't you heard that the post of Messiah has been filled already?'

Jesus saves solo. We place ourselves on dangerous ground when we presume to share his unique role. Our safety consists not in asserting what we will do for him, but in humbly receiving what he alone has done for us.

Father God, reveal our hidden pride by the convicting insight of the Holy Spirit. Give us humility to receive Jesus' work as a gift. May we never attempt to contribute anything to it. Protect us on every side and lead us on level ground today. In Jesus' name. Amen.

Sometimes a single court case can expose the corruption of an entire system. Take, for example, the Gregson v. Gilbert case concerning the slave ship *Zong*. In 1781, one hundred and thirty-three slaves were massacred on board, when the ship's fresh water supplies ran low. To the disgrace of the whole system, the courts didn't hold a murder trial but an insurance hearing.

The British public was aghast that these infinitely precious victims were considered property. As a result, opinion shifted significantly in favour of abolishing the slave trade.

Jesus' trial before the Roman governor, Pontius Pilate, unmasks the evil entrenched within the world's systems of power. We will spend four days on this momentous event. Today, we begin with a sketch of the proceedings.

The Jewish leadership need Pilate to rubberstamp their decision to crucify Jesus (verse 30). Pilate evidently just wants them to go away (verse 31), but he quickly realises that this is not going to happen. They need his permission for the death sentence they seek (verse 31).

Pilate interviews Jesus (verses 33–37) and concludes that there is no case to answer (verse 38). That should end the matter, but Pilate doesn't want to upset the Jewish leaders.

His politically astute mind alights on a way for everyone to win: the annual Passover prisoner release. Pilate hopes that the Jewish leaders will freely choose to release Jesus (verse 39). Instead, they set free Barabbas, a convicted insurrectionist. Meanwhile, the innocent Jesus is flogged (verses 1-3).

Pilate hopes that the flogging might satisfy the religious leadership. He presents the bloodied figure. 'Here is the man!' (verse 5), he declares, as if to say *can this pathetic person really be a threat to you?* The clamour for crucifixion only grows louder (verse 6).

For a third time, Pilate declares Jesus' innocence (verse 6). This prompts the religious leaders to specify their charges at last. Jesus is a religious blasphemer, claiming to be the Son of God (verse 7). And he is a political rebel because his claim to be a king defies Caesar (verse 12).

Amid cries of 'Crucify! Crucify!' Pilate tries desperately to release Jesus one last time. 'Shall I crucify your king?' he implores. Israel's leaders respond with a blasphemous rejection of the rule of God: 'We have no king but Caesar' (verse 15). With that, innocent Jesus is led away to be crucified.

This case rips off the veneer and exposes the rottenness within the political and religious systems of this world. Truth and justice are routinely trampled in a stampede of pride, envy, self-preservation, fear and lies.

If only there was an alternative kingdom to believe in …

Father God, make us as wise as serpents and as innocent as doves. In all our dealings with this world, may we think and act under the authority of Jesus' kingdom, and in the righteousness, peace and joy of the Holy Spirit. In Jesus' name. Amen.

If you had to act the part of Pontius Pilate in a drama, how would you deliver his response to Jesus' claim to be the King of truth: 'What is truth?' (verse 38). I'd inflect the words with a cynical sigh and an edge of derision in my voice.

Politics asks, what *works* to preserve position and increase power? Business asks, what *pays*? As individuals we ask, what will make me *happy*? As for the question of *truth*, well, to those who think like Pilate, it has no relevance in the real world.

One must first establish power, make profit and secure happiness, then truth might be discussed as a matter of speculation. Pilate's court, however, has no place for such trivial matters as what is, and is not, true.

Yet before Pilate stands Jesus Christ who said, 'I am the way and the truth and the life' (14:6).

Pilate has asked Jesus if he is a king (verse 33). Jesus admits that he is, but stresses that his kingdom is from another place, from outside this world (verse 36). His kingdom is not established by force but by the truth its king proclaims. Its subjects are those who listen to the truth (verse 37).

Pilate is completely unimpressed. Truth is nothing to him. It funds no army. It fights no battles. And on the face of it, truth loses. Pilate, the man of political power, is about to crucify the King of truth to satisfy the hard realities of the situation. Truth? Who cares!

But truth has a double destiny.

On the one hand, it is destined to be crucified in every generation. We should not be surprised when God's truth is marginalised, despised and vilified in our own time. Yet, on the other hand, know for sure the truth is destined to be exalted over every generation.

With hindsight, we can see that the King of truth was exalted over Pilate's court. Pilate's name is only known today because of this encounter with Jesus. Indeed, King Jesus still transforms lives by the power of his truth, whereas the politics of Pilate's empire are ancient history.

What is truth? Jesus is the truth, and he is everything.

Lord Jesus, King of truth, once crucified but now exalted over all kingdoms, have mercy on us, deceitful people in a world of lies. May your Spirit captivate our minds and hearts with what is true, noble, right, pure, lovely, admirable, excellent and praiseworthy. For the Father's glory. Amen.

God sometimes puts his own words into the unwitting mouths of people who are working against him. John records several such comments (see, for example, 11:50 and 12:19), including today's text: 'Here is the man!' or, in traditional translation, 'Behold the man!' (verse 5).

We'll consider first what Pontius Pilate means by this declaration, and then what God intends to say.

Pilate is desperate for the Jewish leaders to drop their charges against Jesus, so he displays the prisoner in all his weakness. 'Why be threatened by someone as pathetic as this?' he seems to plead.

When Pilate says, 'Behold the man!', he wants to draw attention to everything that makes Jesus despicable and ludicrous.

This weak man's traumatised body is mantled in a purple cloak. Blood oozes from the crown of thorns that completes a biting parody of kingship. Bruises to his face reinforce an impression of weakness and defeat.

Pilate intends to discredit Jesus and mock his claims. At the same time, God is inviting us to behold his Son's glory.

As Jesus embarked on his suffering, he announced, 'Now the Son of Man is glorified' (13:31). The Son of Man is the title of the king destined to inherit everlasting rule, as representative head over a vast global people. His mission is prophesied in Daniel 7:13–14.

Can we really see the glory of the supreme Son of Man in the stooped figure at this trial? Look carefully.

We see a representative man. Remember that Jesus is now in Barabbas' place. He stands where the condemned criminal should be, securing his undeserved freedom.

We see an innocent man, because at that very moment, Pilate publicly repeats his verdict: 'I find no basis for a charge against him' (verse 4).

We see a royal man. The purple robe and crown of thorns were intended as mockery, but God means them as tokens of Jesus' genuine identity.

'Behold the man!' What do we see as we fix our eyes on Jesus? A suffering man, yes. The blood and bruises are real.

Yet we must also hear God speaking through Pilate's words. Behold, therefore, the Son of Man. Here is the innocent representative of the guilty. He is humbled for that moment, but even then reveals his eternal reign.

Father God, open our eyes to behold Jesus as you intend us to view him. Remove the blindness that prevents our unbelieving friends and family members from seeing who he truly is. In dependence on the convicting and illuminating work of the Spirit, and for the glory of the Son of Man. Amen.

There is nothing remarkable about a defendant condemning the court. Plenty of alleged war criminals have railed against the legitimacy of the court that presumes to try them.

But has anyone ever passed judgement from the dock with the calm authority of Jesus? 'You would have no power over me if it were not given to you from above. Therefore the one who handed me over to you is guilty of a greater sin' (verse 11).

Jesus has remained silent during Pilate's latest round of questioning (verse 9). The judge tries to intimidate the accused into talking with a reminder of exactly how important he is: 'Don't you realise I have power either to free you or to crucify you?' (verse 10)

Jesus could have pointed out the irony of Pilate's boast. In truth, the governor is powerless. His own cowardice before the Jewish leaders deprives him of the freedom to spare an innocent man. Jesus, however, makes no jibe.

Rather, he respectfully acknowledges Pilate's authority over him. It is given from above, not just by Rome, but ultimately by God.

This statement carries two implications. On the one hand, Pilate has a right to pass judgement. On the other hand, he is accountable to God for the judgement he passes. God holds every ruler up to scrutiny, with full knowledge of the responsibility each one bears for history's injustices.

Earlier in John's Gospel, Jesus claimed that the Father had entrusted all judgement to him (5:22–27). It should come as no surprise, then, to hear Jesus pronounce God's meticulous verdict on the present case.

Pilate is guilty, Jesus declares. But greater guilt belongs to the Jewish leaders who handed Jesus over to the Roman governor. They acted with more independent initiative. And they knew more of God's truth.

Jesus' pronouncement on Pilate and the Jewish leaders indicates that the Father has indeed entrusted all judgement to him. Yet again, his glory shines out from the depths of his humiliation. We are watching a preview of the eternal Judge in action.

Lord Jesus, we praise you, whom the Father has appointed the Judge of all people and the Saviour of everyone who puts their trust in you. Fill us with the Holy Spirit and give us humility as we stand in awe of your majesty. For your glory. Amen.

Jesus is required to carry his own cross to the execution site. Its Aramaic name is *Golgotha*, meaning 'The Place of the Skull'. English-speakers know it as Calvary, from the Latin word for skull, *calvaria*. God the Father glorified the Son of Man on this ghastly hill.

Today, we pay close attention to the sign Pilate had written and fastened to the cross. It was common for the charges against a criminal to be specified on a written notice above the crucified person's head. Remarkably, the sign on Jesus' cross states no charge, but only gives a name and a title: 'JESUS OF NAZARETH, THE KING OF THE JEWS' (verse 19).

Pilate's driving motivation for wording the sign like this is his anger against the Jewish leadership. They forced his hand to give them what they wanted. Now, it's his turn to humiliate them.

Perhaps there's a note of insult, as if Pilate is suggesting that this crucified man is just the sort of king they deserve. He clearly intends to cause them significant embarrassment. The Jewish Passover pilgrims flocking into Jerusalem will see the multilingual sign as they enter the city and wonder what on earth is going on: did the Jewish nation receive this man as their king? Is that why Rome killed him?

The Jewish leaders insist on a face-saving change to the sign's wording. They want to make clear that Jesus' claim to kingship has been rejected: 'this man claimed to be king of the Jews' (verse 21).

Pilate is in no mood to spare their blushes. At last, when it costs him nothing, he is resolute and insists that the placard will stand immovable.

Or it is really God who is refusing to budge?

Yet again, the Father is putting his own words into his enemies' unwitting mouths – or, to be more precise, on their signage. God is using Pilate's notice to broadcast the truth that Jesus *is* the King of the Jews.

And not only of the Jews. The fact the sign is written in three languages suggests that his reign extends far beyond Jerusalem.

God will not allow that banner to be altered. It must remain, to testify that Jesus reigns even from the cross. It stands immovable, to declare that this shameful instrument serves – for a few hours – as Christ's glorious throne.

Father in heaven, we praise you that Jesus was lifted to the throne of Calvary. Let us never be ashamed of the cross but, with our minds renewed by the Spirit, may the world be crucified to us and we to the world. In the name of Jesus, the King of the Jews. Amen.

All four Gospels mention the gambling executioners. They played at the foot of the cross for possession of Jesus' seamless undergarment. John gives more information about this incident than Matthew, Mark or Luke. What significance does he see in it?

On one level, it demonstrates human indifference in all its callousness.

How hardened these men must have been to profit from the crucified victim as he suffered before their eyes. They are only concerned about material matters. The *morality* of stealing from the dying man doesn't concern them at all. These rank-and-file soldiers exhibit the same pitiless indifference that facilitates all the atrocities of history.

At a deeper level, the game over the clothes illustrates Jesus' self-offering in all its completeness.

Most paintings of Jesus on the cross preserve his modesty. The soldiers didn't care about that. They took his undergarment and left him naked.

When Adam and Eve turned away from God, nakedness became an outward expression of their inward guilt and shame. On the cross, the Son of God took this disgrace upon himself. He assumed our nakedness so we can be clothed in all his perfect qualities.

On the deepest level, this incident exhibits God's sovereignty in all its power.

In verse 24, John quotes Psalm 22, a song King David wrote 1000 years before Jesus' death. The psalm describes the suffering of God's

Messiah, before prophesying his victory. It mentions the very game John witnessed the soldiers playing.

Why did they play it? The word 'so' in verse 24 leads us to the ultimate reason. The Scripture had to be fulfilled: '*So* this is what the soldiers did' (my emphasis). God's word stated that they would gamble for Jesus' clothing, and so they did. God's sovereign purpose was irresistibly at work.

I remember my amazement when, as a teenager, I first discovered the links between Psalm 22 and Jesus' death. It boosted my confidence that the cross really is at the centre of God's purposes. If you have never read that psalm, I urge you to do so today.

With the perspective of Scripture, we can clearly discern divine glory in this scene. The executioners' game – unbeknown to them – confirms God's faithfulness to his promises. And their cruelty serves to highlight Jesus' infinite love.

Father, we praise you for the fulfilment of your sovereign plan through the death of your Son. Lord Jesus, we thank you for offering yourself for us so completely. Holy Spirit, overcome our callous indifference and clothe us in compassion, kindness, humility, gentleness and patience. In Jesus' name. Amen.

Pain seems to intensify our awareness of ourselves and to accentuate the irritation we feel towards others. Jesus must have been tempted to respond to his own agonies in a self-centred way too. Instead, he kept looking outwards to the needs of others. This is demonstrated in a moving incident John must have treasured.

This beloved disciple stands near the cross. Mary, Jesus' mother, is there too. I find it hard even to imagine her pain as she watched her firstborn son on the cross. Jesus sees their anguish. In compassion he gives Mary and John to one another as mother and son.

This is a unique and intimate incident, involving specific individuals. Even if it has no wider significance than that, it remains an uplifting demonstration of Jesus' love. However, John intends his readers to see in it an illustration of a broader reality.

Jesus forms a new family from his cross. He unites Mary and John to illustrate his intention to draw together all his people into the church.

We naturally see the cross as God's way of restoring our relationship with himself. We are not so used to viewing it as his way of establishing and maintaining our relationships with one another. Yet it is *from the cross* that Jesus establishes his family.

The cross is the foundation of our life together. Later in the New Testament, Paul urges the members of the Ephesian church towards unity. He bases his appeal on Jesus' death, where all the hostility between them was put to death (Ephesians 2:16).

The Lord's Supper stands at the centre of church life as a repeated reminder that our unity is in Jesus' broken body and shed blood.

Jesus didn't only die to save individuals. He offered himself on the cross to form a family, a people, a body. This includes your local fellowship.

Do you belong to one? If not, perhaps you can see why it is so important to get connected. Jesus died to give you a place in his family. It won't help you or honour him if you stay disconnected.

Churches are never perfect because they are populated by flawed people. Don't let the inevitable frustrations hold you back from involvement. Jesus died to draw us together, and his shed blood has not lost its power to bring peace.

Father God, we thank you that Jesus drew us into fellowship with his family through the sacrifice of himself. Open our eyes to recognise fellow believers as your gift to us, and to believe that we are a gift to them too. In the Spirit's power and by virtue of Jesus' offering. Amen.

Jesus promises that those who trust in him will never thirst (4:13–14; 6:35; and 7:37–38). How striking, then, that he should utter the words, 'I am thirsty!' (verse 28).

Jesus' thirst hints at the intensity of the physical horrors he endures as fluids drain from his body. It is likely that John also intends us to detect spiritual significance in it.

Careful readers of verse 28 will notice that John offers two reasons why Jesus says, 'I am thirsty.'

First, he knows that 'everything had now been finished'. His work is done. He knows that, and he wants the world to know it too. Yet he cannot announce the news with a dehydrated mouth. By saying 'I thirst', he is asking for a sip from the nearby jar of wine vinegar. The drink will enable him to utter the words we will consider tomorrow: 'It is finished' (verse 30).

Second, Jesus says that he thirsts 'so that Scripture would be fulfilled'. Two passages of Scripture seem to be in his mind: Psalms 22 and 69.

In Psalm 22, God's rejected King languishes in the dust of death. We read that his tongue sticks to the roof of his mouth, a reference to terrible thirst (Psalm 22:15). Psalm 69 also refers to the suffering of God's anointed King. He is given vinegar for his thirst (Psalm 69:21).

Jesus says, 'I am thirsty' to identify himself as the one described in these psalms. He is directing us to consider their storylines. They both begin with the Messiah's suffering. They both end with his triumph and exultation. For those who have ears to hear, 'I thirst' is a hint of Jesus' coming victory.

These two reasons account for why Jesus says the words 'I thirst'. But why does he enter a state of thirst at all?

Sinners are rightly under God's judgement. Spiritually speaking, we live in a burning desert. We will die of thirst. On the cross, Jesus enters that parched state for us. His cry of 'I am thirsty' outwardly expresses the unseen agony of judgement that he bears for us.

That judgement has past now. Jesus has endured it entirely. As a result, he has accessed for us an endless supply of life-giving water. He promises to pour it into the hearts of all who come to him, by the gift of his Holy Spirit.

Father God, we come to Jesus, who bore our thirst, that we might have living water through the Holy Spirit. Fill us in our emptiness, refresh us in our weariness and satisfy our restless hearts to the praise of all he accomplished on the cross. In his name. Amen.

A sip of wine vinegar gives Jesus enough voice to declare for our benefit what he already knew to be true: 'It is finished' (verse 30).

What is finished? To answer that question, we must recall the prayer Jesus offered the previous evening (17:1–5). In it, he embraced the work the Father had given him to accomplish: to gain eternal life for all his people. Now, he declares this work complete. Eternal life is ours.

We could fill out that answer with reference to other phrases from John's Gospel: love is fully expressed (13:1); the cup of wrath is drained (18:11); Satan is driven out (12:31); and the world is overcome (16:33). All this is done. It will remain irreversibly and forever done.

Other belief systems require us to *do* things if we are to have salvation, in whatever way that might be defined. They say, 'Learn this; sacrifice that; pay the other!' This approach leads to a cycle of fear, resentment and guilt.

There is full relief from all this in Jesus' triumphant declaration, 'It is finished.' He has accomplished our salvation in full and gives it to us as a gift. We don't need to *do* things to achieve God's acceptance. We trust that Jesus has *done* it all.

Evidence to strengthen this confidence quickly comes to light. Note carefully what happens next: 'With that, he bowed his head and gave up his spirit.'

This is not usually how death works. Sinners *must* die. We do not yield our lives freely; they are taken from us.

Jesus is representing humanity in its sinfulness. On the cross he carries such a weight of human evil that Paul can go so far as to say that *he was made sin* for us (2 Corinthians 5:21). Yet at the point of death, he freely yields his life. Why was it not taken from him?

There is a glorious answer, and we know it already: 'It is finished.' Our sin, which he carried, is fully paid for. Death, therefore, cannot seize him. By freely giving up his spirit, Jesus confirms that he bears our guilt no more. And neither do we.

'It is finished.' Take refuge in these impregnable words, no matter what the world, the flesh or the devil may say to undermine your life. Take your stand upon all that Jesus has done for you and be at peace.

Lord Jesus Christ, we thank you for declaring your work complete that your people might rest forever in your victory cry. Have mercy on our unbelieving fear and fill us instead with reassurance from the Holy Spirit. For the glory of the Father whose work you completed. Amen.

John is still standing near the cross when the soldiers arrive with Pilate's permission to break the legs of the crucified victims. This was a usual method for hastening death. With no lower body support to lift the abdomen, the victim quickly suffocated under the weight of the chest.

The soldiers perform this brutal efficiency on the two men executed with Jesus. Coming to him, they suspect that he is already dead. A rough spear thrust confirms it, as blood and water flow from his side.

I will leave the medical explanation for this incident to those qualified to offer it. As far as the soldiers were concerned at the time, the fact Jesus shows absolutely no reaction to the spear thrust confirms beyond doubt that he is dead.

John saw this too. He urges us to believe his testimony. He implores his readers to believe that Jesus really did die. This silences those who claim that the 'resurrection' was nothing more than a remarkable recovery.

Seeing the corpse violently punctured, John beseeches us to accept that our Saviour is fully human. He is not a superhuman apparition, who only appears to be like us. He is a real physical man, saving us from the depths of our fallen human condition.

John also witnesses to God's ongoing commitment to Jesus, even after he has died. The Father fulfils two prophecies through these post-mortem events.

First, he preserves Jesus' bones intact. In the regulations for the Passover, the Israelites were instructed not to break the bones of the sacrificial lamb (Exodus 12:46). As Jesus' legs are spared, John understands that God's ultimate Passover Lamb is suspended, slain, before his eyes.

Second, Jesus' side is pierced. This fulfils the prophet Zechariah's startling promise that one day the Israelites will pierce the Lord himself (Zechariah 12:10). Yes, they will thrust through the living God. Yet, 'On that day a fountain will be opened to the … inhabitants of Jerusalem, to cleanse them from sin and impurity' (Zechariah 13:1).

These prophecies are fulfilled before John's eyes. God is pointing to Jesus as Israel's pierced God and the source of her cleansing and renewal.

John testifies to all this. The prophets also testify. And God the Father appeals to us from the lengthening shadows of Calvary: 'Believe!' he urges us. 'Trust in my beloved Son, and live.'

Our Father in heaven, we believe your testimony about your Son. Apply his cleansing blood to our lives through the sanctifying work of the Spirit. Help us to turn from sin and to love you with all our heart, soul, mind and strength. In Jesus' name. Amen.

With hindsight, we can see that something new is astir from the moment Jesus dies. The hints are faint, like the earliest tremors of a volcano soon to erupt. Even at his burial, it is as if the ground is beginning to quiver.

The stirring is evident in the men who buried Jesus' body: Joseph of Arimathea and Nicodemus. It seems that Jesus' death has not extinguished the faith of these influential men, but ignited it.

John deliberately reminds us of their previous attitudes to Jesus, to highlight the contrast with their new-found boldness.

Joseph had believed in Jesus before, but he kept quiet about it out of fear (verse 38). Now, he blows his own cover. Throwing political caution to the wind, he asks Pilate for permission to bury Jesus.

Nicodemus leaves a fascinating trail through John's Gospel. He 'earlier had visited Jesus at night' (verse 39; see 3:1–2). On that occasion, he came across as patronising and ignorant. In 7:50–51, he gently challenges his powerful colleagues' closed-minded attitude towards Jesus. Now, he makes no secret of his allegiance.

Jesus' death emboldens both men. They willingly associate themselves with him. His shame becomes theirs, as they unpick the nails, splinters and thorns from the corpse.

These two wealthy men honour Jesus. Nicodemus provides spices weighing the equivalent of two full suitcases. The pair embalm their Master and lay him in a brand-new tomb. They give him a burial fit for a king. And through their actions, the Father is reminding us that this is exactly who Jesus is.

This new boldness requires an explanation. Why the rumblings of fresh confidence *before* the Easter Day eruption? God has renewed these men through the events of Jesus' death.

We now know that Jesus is raised from the dead. However, the cross remains our rallying point of defiance against the forces of evil. We reason that, since God's glory shone victorious on that terrible day, there is no future day on which he cannot prevail.

Take courage! Step into the future with the same steady, thoughtful boldness that we witness in these two honoured men.

Almighty Father, we worship you, even in the solemnity of loss and grief. Embolden us to stand unashamed with Jesus, through the life-giving influence of his death. Fill our empty hearts with the Spirit's guarantee that the future belongs to you. For the glory of Christ crucified. Amen.

Jesus Christ is risen today! Death's stranglehold on creation is broken and the future belongs to the once-crucified Son of Man.

Yet on the morning that reordered the universe, faith spluttered only falteringly to life. John's account of the disciples' gradual progress from grief to joy makes me think of three waves breaking successively higher up a beach.

First, Mary Magdalene, straining her eyes in the half-light, sees that the stone covering the mouth of the tomb has been moved (verse 1). Not knowing what to think and still catching her breath from the sprint back to Peter, she can only express her fear: 'They have taken the Lord out of the tomb, and we don't know where they have put him' (verse 2).

Mary had got close enough to the tomb to notice the stone's misplacement, but no closer. Now the second wave breaks. John runs beyond the point at which Mary turned back, beats Peter to the scene and, standing at the entrance, bends down to look inside (verse 5). He notices that the strips of Jesus' burial linen are still in the tomb.

Then the third wave crashes, as Peter rushes past John and bursts into the cave. He is struck by a further detail. The cloth that had shrouded Jesus' head is neatly folded, separate from the other strips of linen. What does it mean?

Only now does John enter the tomb, and finally faith is lit within him (verse 8). He didn't grasp the full meaning of the scene. That would come later as he understood the promises of Scripture (verse 9). At this point, he only knows that Jesus' body cannot have been snatched away.

Two facts make that unlikely. Anyone taking the body, whether friend or foe, would have carried it in its linen coverings. Yet the cloths remained. And what grave robber would have taken care to fold these pieces of fabric? John realises that no one has moved Jesus' body. Could the Master, perhaps, be alive?

Jesus' resurrection transforms everything. Death doesn't have the last word anymore. The universe's future belongs to the Risen One. The disciples had stumbled unwittingly into a new world. Let John's eyewitness account of his early morning discovery confirm you in joyful conviction.

Almighty Father, we praise you for raising Jesus from the dead. By the power of the Holy Spirit, set our hearts ablaze with irrepressible joy. Let the message of the resurrection ring out in this dying world today, bringing many to new life. To the glory of Father, Son and Holy Spirit. Amen.

I have often daydreamed about Mary's personal encounter with the risen Jesus, imagining what it would have felt like to be in her place.

Peter and John have left the tomb, but she stays there to weep. As she stoops down to look inside – perhaps hoping to find a further clue about what has happened – she sees two angels (verses 11–12).

Asked why she is crying, she utters to them the same hopelessly vague explanation she had offered the disciples earlier: 'They have taken my Lord away … and I don't know where they have put him' (verse 13).

Then Jesus himself appears before her and asks the same question as the angels (verses 14–15).

Why doesn't she recognise him? As he approaches, she is looking away from him. Her eyes are filled with tears. And besides, Jesus is a corpse – isn't he? But Mary has been addressed by a living person. He can't be Jesus, by definition. The gardener was a fair guess.

Perhaps John intends us to pick up echoes of Eden, where the Lord God planted a garden (Genesis 2:8). Is there a hint that Jesus is that same divine gardener, now performing a work of recreation?

Just think of the transformation that took place when Jesus spoke Mary's name. As it was in the beginning, so in the Easter garden: the Son of God speaks, and Mary's darkness is turned to light.

No wonder she wants to grasp hold of him and hug him to herself. But she mustn't. He is going to the Father to expand his work through the gift of the Spirit, just as he promised.

John stands alone among the Gospel writers in narrating personal encounters between the risen Jesus and the disciples. He records details of conversations with Mary Magdalene, Thomas and Peter. John is illustrating Jesus' personal interest in meeting every one of us.

Earlier in John's Gospel, our Lord described himself as the Good Shepherd who knows his sheep by name (10:3). He addresses Mary by name, and the implication is that he calls us by name too.

It turns out that daydreaming about this encounter is not fanciful after all. The risen Lord does call each one of his people by name. What's yours? He knows it, calls you by it, and wants to give you the joy of his resurrection.

Father, we praise you that Jesus knows his people by name. Forgive our reticence to receive such love. Renew us by the power of the Holy Spirit that we will live boldly and joyfully in the freedom of the children of God. For Jesus' sake. Amen.

Mary must have told the disciples about her morning encounter with Jesus; how he referred to them as brothers; that he called his Father *their* Father (verse 17). Yet it seems that on Easter Sunday evening they are still in a negative frame of mind, gathered in a locked room 'for fear of the Jewish leaders' (verse 19).

Suddenly, Jesus is there among them.

The doors were locked. We would love to know how he got in! We might learn fascinating things about the nature of his resurrection body. But we are not told. Let's be content simply to know that nothing keeps Jesus from his people.

He bears good news for his fearful friends: every promise he had made to them still stands.

He had promised to overcome the world and to give his followers peace within it (14:27 and 16:33). Now triumphant over death, he twice pronounces peace upon them. In fulfilment of another promise (16:20), this turns their sorrow to joy.

Likewise, he confirms his earlier promise to send them into the world as his witnesses (15:27 and 17:20). Despite their failure during the past days, that plan stands. They will go into the world bearing Jesus' authority.

That's what Jesus means when he talks about them forgiving, or not forgiving, sins (verse 23). It's not that they will have power to determine where other people stand with God. They are authorised to pronounce the verdict God has already passed: that those who trust in Jesus are forgiven.

Best of all, the risen Jesus has not forgotten his many promises about the Holy Spirit. He breathes on his disciples to indicate that he now possesses authority to send the Spirit – although they will have to wait until after his ascension to experience fully what his arrival will mean.

Proverbs 13:12 says, 'Hope deferred makes the heart sick, but a longing fulfilled is a tree of life.' As Jesus resurrects dead hopes, the disciples' sick hearts are healed. Sorrow and fear flee away. They are replaced with confidence and joy.

Jesus promised to be present with his believing people by his Spirit. He is certainly with you now. His risen presence still brings peace to troubled minds and joy to fearful hearts.

Our Father, we confess our failure to follow your Son with faith and obedience. Have mercy on us by his shed blood, and – convinced of his resurrection victory – give us peace, joy and confidence in his presence. By the ministry of the Spirit, and for the glory of Jesus' name. Amen.

I've heard people say that they especially identify with the disciple Thomas. They admire his rational approach to the resurrection. They, too, demand compelling evidence of its truth.

Such friends are right to require compelling reasons to believe. They are equally mistaken to think that Thomas models a reasonable approach to faith.

Thomas was absent when Jesus appeared to the other disciples on Easter Sunday evening, and he refused to accept their report. After all, how could he believe in something that *cannot* happen? Dead bodies do not rise!

But wait – dead bodies can rise, and Thomas had seen it happen. He witnessed Jesus raise Lazarus from the tomb (chapter 11). That experience ought to have opened his mind at least to the possibility that Jesus himself had been raised, as his friends claimed.

Or did he have reason to think that they were lying to him? Surely these friends had given Thomas no just cause for treating them as false witnesses.

Thomas knew, as well as they did, that the tomb was empty, and that Jesus' body was missing. Yet he refuses the one explanation that fits the facts. He rejects it, even though it's offered on the testimony of people he trusts and concerns a person who had demonstrated authority over death.

This supposed icon of intellectual rigour has plenty of evidence, but he refuses to consider it. Thomas ought to be named the Patron Saint of Stubbornness.

He demonstrates his closed-mindedness with his absurd demand for proof. Will he really poke Jesus' wounds? He only offers to do something so grotesque because he is certain that he won't have to do it.

One week later, Jesus appears to his disciples again. Thomas is present this time. He is overwhelmed. He forgets all about prodding the nail marks. The Bible's most famous doubter makes the fullest statement of faith that we find anywhere in John's Gospel: 'My Lord and my God!' (verse 28).

Thomas is offered the evidence he asked for, but he immediately realises that he doesn't need to make full use of it. In fact, he doesn't need it at all. He already has every reason to believe in the resurrection, based on the testimony of the other disciples.

The same is true for everyone. That includes our friends who most identify with Thomas and his famous doubts.

Jesus, Lord and God, forgive our reticence to trust in you, when you have shown yourself to be absolutely dependable. In your mercy, make us clear-headed and wholehearted in our faith. By the Spirit's power and for the Father's praise. Amen.

After Jesus returns to the Father, he will no longer be visible to the world. This means a transition must take place in the way people come to believe in him. Faith grounded in seeing him needs to give way to a faith founded on the testimony of eyewitnesses.

This is the distinction Jesus has in mind in verse 29: 'Then Jesus told [Thomas], "Because you have seen me, you have believed; blessed are those who have not seen and yet have believed."'

Thomas' faith came through seeing Jesus. Yet, in fact, he didn't need visual evidence. The testimony of Jesus himself, along with the witness of the other disciples, should have been compelling enough.

I used to worry that Jesus is encouraging blind faith here. Far from it! Thomas didn't forfeit a blessing because he asked for evidence. The problem was that he refused the testimony of the eyewitnesses, and he demanded a validation that he didn't need.

Thomas' story gives John the perfect opportunity to state his purpose in writing his Gospel. Hundreds of pages could have been written to recount Jesus' miracles and teaching, but John has made a careful selection of seven signs: Water into wine (chapter 2) and the feeding of the 5000 (chapter 6); the healings of the official's son (chapter 4), the lame man (chapter 5) and the blind man (chapter 9); and the raising of Lazarus (chapter 11) and Jesus' own resurrection (chapter 20).

None of John's readers saw these events. Yet John's eyewitness testimony gives every reader sufficient grounds to receive Jesus as

God's global and eternal King (the Christ), who is equal to the Father (the Son of God).

However, John's Gospel aims at far more than persuading us that it is reasonable to trust in Jesus. John wants us to experience what can only be received by faith: Jesus' risen life.

Perhaps you don't believe, yet. Then read John's Gospel from the beginning with the author's aim in mind. I pray that God's Spirit will bring you to new life, through the narratives John selected with such care.

Or perhaps you do believe and you long to experience Jesus' life more abundantly. Return to the apostolic testimony every day. Take Jesus at his word. Bank on his many promises and expect that the Spirit will fulfil them in you.

Father God, empower us by the Spirit to trust that Jesus is, to us, everything he has promised to be: the Bread of life, the Light of the world, the True Vine, the Gate, the Good Shepherd, the Resurrection, the Way, the Truth and the Life. And so, may we experience his fullness always. In his name. Amen.

'Perhaps when you read this story, you glowed, and called those happy who were with him ...' So wrote John Chrysostom, the fourth-century preacher, whose great gifts gained him the nickname 'Golden Mouth'.[6]

I am one of those readers. I do glow as I imagine what it must have been like to share in this breakfast barbeque. Just picture being there on the beach with the risen Jesus in the dawn half-light, the fish already cooking on the crackling fire. I'd want it to go on forever.

What is the significance of this encounter, beyond providing further evidence of Jesus' resurrection?

First, Jesus teaches a vital lesson about the disciples' future success.

Luke's Gospel contains the account of an incident like this one. It's from the early days of the disciples' adventures with Jesus (Luke 5:1–11). The young rabbi commissions the professional fishermen as 'fishers of people'. It is vital for them to learn how this new kind of fishing works.

For a whole night they apply their expert skill, without success. Then, at the command of the risen Lord, they take the haul of their lives. The lesson is that success in the future mission will depend on obedience to the risen Jesus.

Second, Jesus sounds a sobering echo of past failure – Peter's in particular.

---

6 From John Chrysostom's homily on John 21, available at biblehub.com/commentaries/ chrysostom/John/21

The lakeside setting is reminiscent of Peter's original call. How spectacularly he has messed up since then! And now he sits by a charcoal fire, as he did on the night he denied Jesus.

These are uncomfortable reminders. Little does Peter realise that Jesus is carefully creating the right setting in which to address these past failures and to restore him.

Third, Jesus serves up a mouth-watering foretaste of eternal fellowship.

This breakfast cannot last forever. Jesus will soon return to the Father. Physically absent, he will send the Spirit to bring his presence to the disciples. However, one day, bodily fellowship will be resumed. The breakfast on the beach is a signpost to that eternal fellowship.

This was certainly the conviction of the golden-mouthed Chrysostom. Looking back to the beach barbeque, he couldn't help looking ahead: '[If we] glowed and called those happy who were with him ... consider how great it will be to see him in a body that will never die and enjoy that bliss which passes all language.'

Father in heaven, increase our longing for Jesus' coming – even as you make us more aware of his presence with us now. So set us aglow with anticipation of the fellowship to come, that we might not consider our present struggles worth comparing with the coming glory. In Jesus' name. Amen.

What's massive and deafening, yet invisible and silent?

An elephant in the room.

This is John's third account of a meeting between the risen Jesus and his disciples. With every meeting, the elephant in the room gets bigger and louder: *is someone going to mention Peter's denials?*

I think that if I were in Peter's shoes, I would be aching to raise the matter, to apologise and to clear that air. How would you initiate that conversation, though?

In John 10, Jesus identified himself as the Good Shepherd. Here we see him at work, restoring his wayward sheep.

The setting is designed to relay the foundations of Peter's discipleship. It takes him back to the circumstances of his first encounter with Jesus – the shores of the Sea of Galilee with boats and fishing nets all around.

The conversation restores Peter, failure by failure. He denied Jesus three times, so the Good Shepherd gives him three opportunities to express his love. It's a painful process because, to Peter, the repeated question implies that Jesus doesn't believe him (verse 17).

Why does Jesus put Peter through this? Picture the denials as three gaping ruptures in the hull of a ship. With every declaration of love, each hole is mended until the listing ship floats again.

The Good Shepherd not only gives Peter these precious opportunities to put the past straight. He looks ahead to Peter's future role too:

'Feed my lambs' (verse 15); 'Take care of my sheep' (verse 16); 'Feed my sheep' (verse 17).

The flock will always belong to Jesus. As Peter himself puts it later, Jesus is the Chief Shepherd (1 Peter 5:4). Peter is to be an under-shepherd, feeding the flock with Jesus' living word and defending it against wolves. This will finally cost him his life (verses 18–19).

A radically transformed Peter emerges from this encounter. He is restored, but humbled. His hot-headed self-confidence gives way to dependence that says, 'Lord, you know all things' (verse 17). The leader has reconnected with his identity as – at heart – nothing more than one of the sheep.

I wonder how the Good Shepherd is working in you. It would be helpful to pray quietly, in the light of Peter's reinstatement, and ask him to lead you forward too.

Good Shepherd, lead us safely forward according to your infinite wisdom and compassion. Direct our steps by the word you have spoken and the Sprit you have given, forgiving all that is past and renewing us for whatever lies ahead. To the Father's glory. Amen.

A sideways glance can lose a sprinter the race and deflect a follower of Jesus Christ from the unique course he has set before them. Yet it is very tempting to concern ourselves with whatever gifts, opportunities and calling Jesus might have given to others.

This is Peter's mistake. He notices John, 'the disciple whom Jesus loved' (verse 20), walking closely behind as he talks with Jesus. Jesus has just laid Peter's calling before him. But the newly reinstated leader can't resist taking a sideways glance: 'Lord, what about him?' (verse 21).

In response Jesus effectively says to Peter not 'mind *your* own business', but 'mind *my* own business'. Jesus will shepherd John. How he does so is up to him. Peter has enough to think about as he walks his own unique path of discipleship (verse 22).

In one sense, we should be deeply concerned about the progress of others in their Christian lives. This is an essential quality for every Christian worker. So why was it wrong for Peter to express an interest in Jesus' dealings with John?

We tend to glance sideways for the unworthy purpose of comparing ourselves to others. We would like to know what Jesus has given to them, so we can compare it with what he has given to us.

The result is either pride or discouragement. Both are poisonous to our faith. Both hinder us from running the race that Jesus has wisely and lovingly set before us.

It seems that the early church was as prone to this mistake as we are today (verse 23). Jesus intended his comment about John's future to stop Peter from speculating about God's dealings with others. How ironic that this comment was itself turned into a speculative rumour about John!

I have my race to run. The Shepherd is leading me through his chosen terrain with the resources he has decided to give to me. The same Shepherd leads you too, exactly as he sees fit in his wisdom and love. Stay focused on following him where he has placed you, and resist every temptation to snatch that debilitating sideways glance.

Our Father in heaven, we thank you for giving Jesus to be the Shepherd and Overseer of each of our lives. Give us contentment with the gifts and opportunities he has given us, and may we experience his presence with us now by the power of the Spirit he promised. In Jesus' name. Amen.

10 Publishing

10Publishing is committed to publishing
quality Christian resources that are biblical,
accessible and point people to Jesus.

www.10ofthose.com is our online
retail partner selling thousands of
quality books at discounted prices.

For information contact: **info@10ofthose.com**
or check out our website: **www.10ofthose.com**